ADVANCED PRAISE FOR
UNCOVERING TREASURES THAT MATTER

Every conscientious therapist seeks to be more effective with their clients.

This is a rare book that will make you a better therapist – AND give you an avenue to increase your income. How good is that?

It takes enormous creativity to generate so many insightful questions about key areas of our client's lives. The authors have nailed it. Their key questions illuminate hidden paths to greater wisdom and richer lives. You can now glean their wisdom from decades of private practice to enrich your client's lives – and your own. They are selling clinical diamonds for pennies. Get it now. You and your clients will profit enormously.

~Peter Pearson, Ph.D.
Co-founder of The Couples Institute, and trainer of couple's therapists in 96 countries.

At my age of 85, I find myself increasingly fascinated by the arc of each individual life! For me, each narrative is unique and priceless – and to be treated as the treasure that it is. I see Dr. Bernell and Dr. Svensson's book as providing a thought-provoking collection of what I would call life prompts. These questions and suggestions provide a variety of ways to begin exploring the arc of your own life, to discover your own treasure, and to work creatively with your own unique narrative.

~Sidra Stone, Ph.D.
Co-creator of Voice Dialogue
Author, *The Shadow King: The Invisible Force That Holds Women Back*

Stories about ourselves, how we lived in the past, what is happening in the present, and how we see our future, are the essence of the human imagination. Using those stories to understand ourselves at a deep level and to see our life trajectory and potential is the creative contribution of *Uncovering Treasures That Matter*. We recommend this innovative process to therapists who want to experiment with something new and to clients who want to make deeper sense of their life experience.

~Harville Hendrix, Ph. D. and Helen LaKelly Hunt, Ph. D.
Co-authors, *Getting the Love You Want: A Guide for Couples*

Uncovering Treasures That Matter, a gem that is practical and grounded in research. This is a turn-key manual for therapists—beginners and experienced, to uncover stories that may be hidden but come to life through writing—created by two seasoned professionals, one a psychologist and the other a gerontologist.

The 50 themes provided for problem-solving-centered writing, whether in groups or individually, are exhaustive. The authors have skillfully explored all imaginable scenarios to cue therapists and evoke participant involvement. I highly endorse this book.

~**Francine Toder, Ph.D.**
Psychologist
Author, *Inward Traveler: 51 Ways to Explore the World Mindfully*

Drs. Bonnie Bernell and Cheryl Svensson have produced an excellent and innovative tool for psychotherapists and their clients. *Uncovering Treasures That Matter* explores evidence-based storytelling methods to help clients grow and achieve their goals in psychotherapy. Our lives are stories we repeatedly tell ourselves about our origins, preferences, challenges, traumas, victories, loves, and losses. You are not only the writer of the story that is your life but also the main character, the editor, and the publisher. Your ability to write and revise your life story to reflect strengths and resilience, triumphs and tribulations, adventures, and tragedies, to achieve a sense of satisfaction and completion are the hallmarks of successful therapy.

Expressive writing, whether in journaling, letter writing, short story, or book writing, provides an excellent vehicle for personal growth that I have witnessed in clients of mine. Writing these days appears to consist of 280-character Tweets, brief text, or emails full of abbreviations, slang, emojis, and images. Convincing clients to take the time and invest the effort to sit down and write about their personal experiences and inner lives, to reflect, re-write and edit and revise, and then share with their therapist the results can be challenging. But the results are often amazing. I encourage you to read and learn about the techniques outlined in *Uncovering Treasures That Matter* and then write and encourage your clients to write. You'll discover the transformative power of storytelling.

~**Paul J. Marcille, Ph.D.** Licensed Psychologist Past President of the Santa Clara County Psychological Association Past President of the California Psychological Association Northern California Federal Advocacy Coordinator, American Psychological Association
dr.paulmarcille@gmail.com

The authors of *Uncovering Treasures That Matter* have developed a workbook that will be very helpful to therapists. It presents 50 writing themes that can assist clients in exploring their issues along with vignettes and examples from their clinical practice. This will be a valuable addition to therapists in many different settings who can use writing to help their clients heal, grow and develop.

~**Nina W. Brown, Ed.D., LPC, NCC**
American Psychological Association Fellow
American Group Psychotherapy Association Distinguished Fellow
Professor and Eminent Scholar at Old Dominion University, Norfolk, VA
nbrown@odu.edu

Uncovering Treasures that Matter is an essential guide for any therapist. You may be inspired to include writing directly into sessions or integrate the questions from this book into standard talk therapy. The case studies are helpful guides for any therapist hoping to learn new approaches. The section on talents can help any therapist balance the need for problem-solving with the need to support the client's confidence in their resources to solve those problems. It is an inspiring and engaging read that is an *essential* roadmap for any therapist, teacher, writer, or parent. Wow, I love this book!

~**Lara Honos-Webb, Ph.D.**
Licensed Psychologist
drhonoswebb@gmail.com

Uncovering Treasures That Matter is an incredibly versatile book for therapists, clients, and anyone interested in self-exploration. Beautifully and sensitively written, Drs. Bernell and Svensson have given readers the tools for deeper awareness and understanding and to nudge readers toward committed action that aligns with their new knowledge. For therapists, Bernell and Svensson anticipate the information needed to use TTM in their practices and lay out the specifics in clear and concise language. The book offers not just something for every reader but *many* things to every reader.

~**Robin S. Rosenberg, Ph.D., ABPP**
Licensed Psychologist
Author, *Abnormal Psychology*

This outstanding book, *Uncovering Treasures That Matter,* will now be the primary resource material for my guided integrative therapy groups. It would also be ideal for grounded theory research, facilitating thick and rich content to identify recovery patterns, resilience, and growth. The authors' discernment in producing an essential tool for therapists, clearly the fruits of their life's work, will serve the therapeutic community well.

~ Deena Gayle Hitzke, MAHR, MAPC, Ed.D., LAC

Uncovering Treasures That Matter is an effective, practical, creative way to help clients look deeper, reframe current issues in the context of their life, and receive the help that many need to be self-reflective. This book is an excellent addition to every clinician's toolbox.

~I. David Marcus, Ph.D.
Licensed Psychologist
Silicon Valley Psychological & Consulting Services, Inc.

Between the covers of this beautiful book, Drs. Bonnie Bernell and Cheryl Svensson give the reader access to a vast and all too frequently overlooked gift: a straightforward, enlivening way to an examined life. Like midwives to our lives and their meaningful moments, they provide easy-to-follow, lighthearted, and sensitizing prompts, assignments, and tools that each of us can use to view, review, and deepen our life experiences and their meaning. Their tools invite and encourage us to zoom out and into our lives in a way we would not organically discover without their wise stewardship. As a clinician and a person who wants to look at the treasures of my life, I am grateful for this guide to examine our lives, the treasures/the stories that matter most. Open this book on any page, and your life will be enhanced and enriched. Savor the experience, too.

~Adam Dorsay, Psy.D.
Licensed Psychologist
Psychologist and host of the SuperPsyched Podcast
www.DrAdamDorsay.com

This impressive book, clear and specific, offers any therapist material to use with their clients. The information is sensitively and systematically presented, making it user-friendly and accessible. Bonnie and Cheryl have created an in-depth and creative guide, a compassionate and directed method for thinking in new ways to learn more about yourself.

~**Jennifer Rosenberg, M.A., MFT**
Licensed Marriage Family Therapist

A veritable treasure house of possibilities for therapists to explore the reflective, transformative, and healing potential of writing for those with whom they work — whether individuals, couples, or groups— comprehensive, well-organized, authoritative, and very readable.

~**Philip Holden, Ph.D.** (English Literature)
Registered Clinical Counsellor

As I reflected upon the experiences of the workshops in their entirety, I was overwhelmed by the incredible impact they have had on me. In thinking back on my life experiences, I could not find any event that was more meaningful and life alternating in the most positive way than the collective experiences of these workshops. Once again, thank you for the gift of those experiences. Through your guidance and support, you gave me the courage to explore and uncover priceless truths that might have remained buried in the past without your amazing questions. With gratitude.

~**A note from a participant in many workshops**
Name withheld, by choice.

This book is dedicated to each person who told me what matters to them,
the sine qua non, without which not, of this project.

BLB

To everyone who has written and shared their stories with me –
now I am built to last.

CMS

Uncovering Treasures That Matter
A Therapist's Guide to Asking the Right Questions
An evidence-based writing method
for self-discovery, growth, and healing

Bonnie Bernell, author, *Bountiful Women.* BonnieBernell.com.
Cheryl Svensson, author, with Richard Campbell, *Writing Your Legacy.*
guidedautobiography.com
Cover design and illustration: Bonnie Bernell and Caroline Mustard
Interior graphics: Caroline Mustard

ISBN 978-1-66787-154-7
eBook ISBN 978-1-66787-155-4

Ordering information.

Please get in touch with Bonnie Bernell at blbernell@gmail.com or BookBaby.com to purchase copies of this book.

Disclaimer.

Our heartfelt appreciation goes out to each person who spoke to us about their lives through their stories. We hear the chorus of their voices and wisdom in our heads, cheering each other on. We are awed and honored by their experiences, imagination, and the poignancy of what they had to say. This process of discovery has been a privilege. We received permission to tell each story and changed details to protect their privacy. In addition, we have used the term client to include patient.

Uncovering Treasures That Matter

A Therapist's Guide to Asking the Right Questions

An evidence-based writing method
for self-discovery, growth, and healing

Bonnie Bernell, Ed.D.

Cheryl Svensson, Ph.D.

TABLE OF CONTENTS

PART FOUR: APPENDICES 163

PREFACE

Coming to see a therapist is an act of courage, sometimes with hope and optimism, sometimes with desperation and fear. As a therapist, you want to help your clients get to a better place. To do so, you must reach into yourself and find substance to help them achieve fresh insights. As necessary, you must find techniques to help your clients remember and act on their deepened self-awareness in your sessions.

Uncovering Treasures That Matter (TTM) is a theme-based writing method to help your clients grow. A therapist can use this evidence-based protocol to help clients discover insights and new meanings in their self-discovery process.

The TTM method blends the power of expressive writing, journaling, and life theme writing. It is direct and effective. Why? Stories are what people remember. Just as children are given fables, fairy tales, and parables because these types of stories convey crucial life guidance in the form of easy-to-remember stories, so can stories written and shared with a therapist help clients find clarity and meaning. Stories have been human beings' most reliable means of retaining and sharing information since our early origins.

Bonnie, a licensed psychologist — with decades in private practice, has seen therapists use stories to deliver guidance in a way that people can hear, hold, and use. The TTM method gives therapists another way to use stories, primarily by helping people recall stories concerning the issue that brought them to therapy. That experience can set a client on a new path and help that person stay the course. Stories help people hold onto their enhanced awareness.

Bonnie witnessed the power of stories to change lives when spouses Linda and Dan took part in one of her TTM workshops. The first story Dan wrote altered the trajectory of their marriage. Here is their story.

> **Stories are what people remember.**

In the first week of the workshop, Bonnie assigned each participant to write on a Treasure That Matters – a person, an experience, a thing – and be prepared to read to the group. The next time the group met, Dan volunteered to go first. With his treasured "thing" in hand, he held up a pair of genuinely grungy, worn-out, old shoes that looked horrible and began to read.

Dan came from a poor family. The first pair of new shoes he had ever owned was given to him by his parents when he graduated from high school. He went to a military academy; at graduation, he got special permission to wear those shoes, at that point somewhat worn, to one of the celebrations. At his marriage to Linda, he insisted on wearing those now-very-tired-looking shoes. That began a decades-long battle between Dan and Linda over when and where he would wear those increasingly dreadful shoes. When each of their sons was born, Dan wore those shoes to the hospital to greet the new child. Dan insisted on wearing those shoes when each of his children got married.

They went to couples therapy over those grungy shoes. Linda felt Dan was disrespectful and uncaring to her when he would not stop wearing those shoes on important occasions. Dan felt Linda was controlling and demanding. More therapy. All to no avail. Nothing shifted – until Dan read his story that day in the workshop. When Dan was allowed to tell his story about those shoes, he expressed thoughts he did not even realize he had. Those grungy shoes were a meaningful expression of support from his parents, shoes that made him remember his parents' sacrifices and their expression of love for him. Until that moment, he had never been able to tell his wife the power of those shoes. By the end of his story, Linda was in tears. Each person in the group that day was in tears. For decades the couple had fought. Writing one short story changed everything. Of course, the horrible shoes he brought to class were those very shoes.

Cheryl, with a Ph.D. in psychology, a gerontologist, and director of the Birren Center for Autobiographical Studies, has trained nearly 600 group leaders to offer Guided Autobiography groups, one of the methods from which we have developed Uncovering Treasures That Matter. Cheryl has experienced how writing short autobiographical essays on themes about everyday life experiences help people find new insights and guidance for themselves. For Bev, a participant in one of Cheryl's Guided Autobiography groups, writing and receiving group feedback proved to be life-altering. Here is her story.

Bev was in her late 70s when she joined one of Cheryl's groups. She held on to a grievance from a painful divorce. As the ten-week workshop passed, no matter the week's writing prompt, she brought that grievance into her story. She had married just before her husband was deployed overseas during WWII. When he came home, she went to work, teaching and raising their two sons so that he could finish college and go on to post-graduate work to become a municipal judge. Just as Bev was beginning to reap the benefits, with more money, a bigger home, and the boys in school, her husband divorced her for his secretary. It is an all-too-familiar story, but one that Bev carried like a badge of victimhood. Each week she shared stories about the hurt, anger, and betrayal she felt. No one in the group told her, "Get over it! This happened more than thirty years ago!" But as the end of the workshop neared and the prompt was about spirituality and the meaning of life, Bev experienced an epiphany. "I realized we never had the same values!" she told the group. Bev set herself free of her past. Her whole demeanor lightened. She started traveling. She developed a deep relationship with another older man. Cheryl's Guided Autobiography group supported her into wholeness while she wrote herself into self-discovery.

A written story led Linda and Dan to a more resilient marriage. A written story led Bev from "poor me" to expanded horizons. Time and again, we've both seen stories help clients make a shift to a new trajectory. We have combined the power of storytelling, writing, and therapy with the Uncovering Treasures That Matter method.

You hold in your hands a turnkey workbook. We've provided everything you need, from how to use the TTM method with individual clients, couples, group sessions, and one-day workshops. There are 50 themes with sensitizing questions and prompts to help clients explore their issues through writing. Copy the pages you want your client to have and let them explore the questions. Here are their instructions.

"Ask yourself each question offered. Consider responding to a question(s) that makes you smile, that you are attracted to answering, and to one or two you don't like or want to turn away from. Facing what you don't like, or are uncomfortable with, is often a path to the most significant learning. These questions are guides to prime or stimulate your memories and thoughts about your life. The questions are not intended to be answered in a literal manner. Read through each of them and react to the one(s) that open windows for you. Each life is unique, and the priming questions impact each of us differently."

We have chosen not to use gender-neutral pronouns. We understand this is a profound and meaningful concern, that is, to use language that is gender neutral. At the time of our writing, how these pronouns are to be used is still in flux. With our desire to be inclusive and respectful to a broad audience, some of whom prefer gender-neutral pronouns, and some who are not yet familiar with or understand this change in our use of language, we ask you to understand our decision.

We invite you to explore how to make the Treasures That Matter method a part of your clinical practice. Read on to discover the essence of the method, what's included in different formats, and how to get started.

INTRODUCTION

Uncovering Treasures That Matter (TTM) is a workbook that provides a proven writing method to enhance your therapist's toolkit. This is not a template that must be followed precisely but a writing tool for you to use in different therapy settings. TTM works well in individual counseling sessions, with couples, in workshops, and with groups. It can be easily incorporated into your clinical practice. You may have a client you have been working with for some time. You know them and understand there may be a problem from their early childhood that is impacting them adversely in the present. Look at the themes in Part Three and see if they might hold the key to the problems they are experiencing. There are many themes, all with sensitizing questions and prompts for you to access and use with your clients. You choose the theme and questions that your clinical experience and intuition tell you may help the most with what your client is facing. When they read through the questions and write on one of them, they may discover a part of their past that keeps them from living the life they choose now. Personal writing allows them to select the question and write a response that leads them on a self-discovery journey to a fuller, more satisfying life.

It also works exceptionally well in small group settings where all members grapple with similar therapy concern—for instance, relationship problems. Specifically, each group session focuses on a different aspect of relationships, and members receive a new theme and sensitizing questions to write and answer. They are guided to look deeply within and through their writing and discover the internal blocks that may prevent them from forming relationships of the depth they desire. In the group session, through the guidance of the therapist and the supportive feedback from other group members, they gather insights and begin to heal.

Uncovering Treasures That Matter – is your tool kit to help you and your clients find and write their important stories. This is an evidence-based writing method for self-discovery, growth, and healing. The heart of the book is the 50 themes with associated sensitizing questions and prompts. *You can jump right to the themes—in Part III and offer in full the theme you feel is relevant to your client —or, with your skills, choose the questions you think would be most impactful.* There are many different ways to use this book. Part I introduces the why and how of writing and describes the therapeutic value of writing to heal. The TTM method of questions and writing are described, and examples of how it works in clinical practice. Part II provides the various formats and ways that therapists can use TTM in their practice; this includes individual therapy, work with couples, groups, and one-day workshops. In Part III, you are introduced to the 50 TTM themes in categories for easier reference. The ten categories encompass clinical issues your clients may present, for example, issues regarding transitions, relationships, health, and well-being. The Appendices have all the handouts for you to use to support your clinical process. *Uncovering Treasures That Matter* gives you the tools necessary to help your clients move to a more choice-full life. Time to read on and get started!

Part One:
THE WHY AND HOW OF WRITING

WRITING AS A TOOL FOR HEALING

When you write, you know that you must clearly state to the reader precisely what you mean to say if you want them to understand your message. There is no chance to add explanatory asides; every aspect of the writing must be carefully thought through as one puts pen to paper. This act activates different areas of the brain to examine all the information you wish to convey. It helps to describe the characters, their relationships and feelings, and their varying perspectives. All this is done in the brain, forging new connections and insights. New insights often emerge from the very act of writing them down. You may gain a more profound knowledge of yourself by logically going through the event in your mind. Writing will provide insights that may lead to a deeper understanding of your behavior, emotions, and motivations. It can be a powerful tool for change.

Writing can give meaning to your feelings; when you write and read aloud what you have written, you share that feeling with another person. It helps to gain an understanding of memories and unresolved issues. You will learn new things about yourself and see life differently…all steps to change. The writing process is therapeutic; you will connect with others and yourself by sharing the stories.

In contrast, when we just tell a story, we are resaying what we already know. We watch to see if the other person gets it. We've all heard the 'fish that got away' story repeatedly. Maybe we are even guilty of telling one ourselves. When we write, we create something entirely new. We take those random, unconnected thoughts, write them down, read them over, and rewrite them until we get them right. The next step is to read it to a sensitive and empathetic listener, someone you can dialogue with to gain a more profound knowing. You are transformed in the process of writing, and you see your path more clearly.

> **James Baldwin said about writing, "You go into a book, and you're in the dark, really. You go in with a certain fear and trembling. You know one thing. You will not be the same person when this voyage is over. But you don't know what's going to happen to you between getting on the boat and stepping off. And you have to trust that."**

JOURNAL WRITING

Diaries and journal writing have been around for centuries; this is a private, uncensored examination of one's life – written for oneself. It can take many forms, daily musings, writing to help work through and clarify existing problems, or writing to chronicle one's life. The primary component is private, personal, unstructured, and individual. Ira Progoff was one of the first to identify the value of the journal writing method in his book, *At a Journal Workshop* (https://intensivejournal.org/Intensive_quick-summary.php). He was a psychotherapist who focused on depth psychology and Jungian approaches to study the lives of ordinary people. This method consists of specific writing exercises that touch on all aspects of life. The purpose is for patients to get to know and understand their lives and to find a way to work through whatever issues prevent them from achieving their full potential.

Example: *Where has the time gone? Where has my life gone? In many ways, it feels unplanned but not meaningless. Instead, it seems that one thing naturally unfolds into the next. Primarily it concerns my work and the meaning I gain from that. Without that, I don't know how I would handle the lockdown that COVID has inflicted on all of us. I wonder what my life will be like when I am not working. I wonder if I should think about that now, plan, and listen to what other people say. Not much would happen if I had to figure out what to do and what I care about each day. I think I could wander around. This seems important to me to know.*

EXPRESSIVE WRITING

This method of writing is personal and emotional and uncovers the inner thoughts and feelings related to an event with no regard for "writing style." James Pennebaker began studying expressive writing and wellness in the 1980s with college students at the University of Texas at Austin (https://liberalarts.utexas.edu/psychology/faculty/pennebak). The findings showed that the students who had written about a traumatic event, compared to those who wrote about an emotionally neutral topic, made fewer visits to the health center in the ensuing months (Pennebaker & Beall, 1986). This initial study has led to a plethora of research that shows a range of benefits from expressive writing, such as enhanced immune function, clinical improvement in health status for patients with asthma and rheumatoid arthritis, and improved quality of life for cancer patients (Baikie & Wilhem, 2005). The bottom line is that writing from the heart to the emotional core of things is good for you.

Example: *I'm sitting in a waiting room at a Kaiser facility after receiving the first dose of the COVID vaccine. I have read all the disclaimers regarding this Pfizer vaccine and almost changed my mind. I've now taken a dose of a vaccine that has not been thoroughly tested or 100% approved by the FDA that may prevent COVID but has no tested effect on the new virulent strains of COVID. This is all new and untested, and I have joined the millions who are getting the vaccine to hopefully restore a bit of human contact and freedom into our lives.*

MORNING PAGES

In her book, *The Artist's Way*, Julia Cameron created a writing method she calls morning pages (https://juliacamerononlive.com/the-artists-way/). It is an unstructured form of writing that taps into the subconscious. The process includes three handwritten pages of stream of conscious writing done first thing each morning, thus the title, morning pages. The goal is to get the thoughts out of one's mind and down on paper. It is a cleansing and healing written form of meditation. It was initially designed for blocked artists to get them back to their creative essence and away from the fears that limit them. It applies to everyone. The primary goal is to write without thought for purpose, structure, format, or to share with anyone else. It is written for your eyes only. The desired outcome is a clearing of your mind.

Example: *August 2018, It is 18 degrees centigrade, with clear skies and no wind. I feel like a sailor, reporting on the sailing weather for the day. I rarely think about the weather when I am home in California, mainly because I am not outside in it as I am here in Sweden. And secondly because it seldom changes. If one were to say it will be in the mid-70s F, more than 50% of the time, it would be spot on! Now the laundry is done, and the house is getting back in shape after hosting the family for 2+ weeks. Now I feel the space I need to concentrate and work on meaningful projects. Oh, how I look forward to that.*

LIFE STORY THEMATIC WRITING

In the mid-1970s, while dean of the Leonard Davis School of gerontology at the University of Southern California (USC), James E. Birren created a life story writing method called Guided Autobiography. This method is described in detail in his last book, Telling the Stories of Life in Guided Autobiography Groups (Birren & Cochran, 2001).

(www.guidedautobiography.com). This process guides participants through major life themes using sensitizing questions designed to stimulate their memories. Students must write two pages of their own life story based on one of the questions that resonate with them. In the structured Guided Autobiography (GAB) workshop, participants are divided into small groups of 6 and share their stories. These stories may never have been told, yet each carries such a weight; they are pivotal life events. The program consists of nine life themes and questions each person responds to in writing and then reads to others in their group. GAB was designed as a small group process to help others write their life story two pages at a time.

EXAMPLE: FAMILY—MY HERO. GRACE

She came into my life when I was four. She was an African American lady. I never even thought of her as black; even now, I think of our skin as the same even though I am a fair, white-skinned person. I loved her with all my heart. I still love her. I miss her so much. She died in 1972 when I was 25. I was so distraught that I could not even go to the service.

Grace taught me almost everything that matters in life. She taught me to laugh, sing, dance, and care about other people truly and deeply. She had had a hard life being a black woman in the south. She came north to New Jersey, where I lived. She took such good care of me. My physician father and fashion model mother were busy elsewhere.

Grace was steady. Grace was calm. Grace was good. Grace was brilliant, not educated, but so intelligent. Grace knew what was necessary. Grace's love was of profound importance to my life.

THE TREASURES THAT MATTER METHOD

Therapists use many different methods when helping their clients; one of them may include writing. Many writing traditions have been used for therapeutic healing, including— Journal writing, expressive writing, morning pages, and life-theme writing. They each have their strengths and uses, and we have borrowed from all of them to create the Treasures That Matter writing method.

The Treasures That Matter (TTM) method is a new way for therapists to incorporate writing into their clinical practice. It is an easy method to add to a therapist's tool kit to help clients make unexpected self-discoveries. It is a writing method that focuses on problems or the therapy concern that brought them into therapy and is accompanied by writing prompts that may help clients uncover insights into the struggles they may be facing.

> **Every therapist knows the enormous value of finding and asking the right question to stimulate an awakening, understanding, or aha moment with a client. With TTM, each issue is accompanied by many questions to get to the root of the problem.**

The clients, on their own and in their own time, are asked to read over the questions and select one that resonates with them or speaks to them in a way that opens an inner dialogue. They then write whatever comes up for them, based on the question they chose, in an uncensored, stream-of-conscious manner. This writing begins the journey of therapeutic healing. The writing is shared with the therapist, one-on-one or in a small group setting, and the magic begins. New insights are revealed, feedback and comments help to clarify the past, and a new path forward is discovered. The actual 'Treasures That Matter' is uncovered and leads to further growth and self-understanding.

As a therapist, learning new methods and introducing new material into your therapy practice is always challenging. Finding what is just right for you, the therapist, is critical for anything to work well. You might be the therapist who wants to look at the questions yourself and choose what you believe will be most helpful or productive. Writing, the TTM style, can be more directed and focused according to your preferences as a therapist. Whatever works for you is what to do.

The benefit of having the TTM themes outlined, with the many prompts, is having what you may need ready and at hand.

> **Few among us can generate everything we may need at a particular moment, on the spot, for any client who comes to us.**

The well-researched protocol of writing, reading, and receiving support is a considered and careful psycho-therapeutic intervention that can be profound, meaningful, helpful, and revealing. This is content. This is psychoeducational. This may be a process, too, depending on how you use it. TTM offers another well-considered, expansive, evidence-based protocol that gives you more choices to do your work well.

You know lots of things that help your clients. You are educated, experienced, have had supervision, or are gathering those pieces to be the therapist you want to be. Having taught graduate school, offered supervision, mentored new career therapists, and more, I see that almost every one of us has our heart in the right place and wants to help.

> **Sometimes, that help emerges from within us with ease and comfort. We just know that what we do is what needs to happen, however, we work. Sometimes, however, even the most experienced among us will think, "What can I say or do to help?"**

For each of us, this novel approach, TTM, based on the work of wise teachers before us and now expanded, deepened, and detailed is a missing piece to have in our toolbox. Through considering, writing, reading, being witnessed, supported, and appreciated, in a well-planned and thoughtful way, your client can get expanded help.

> **TTM works because it accesses many elements of what excellent therapy offers—learning, insight, exploration, self-reflection, support and guidance, wisdom from within and from the therapist, safety, and meaningful material for the ongoing life ahead.**

As with any therapeutic intervention, many versions can and do work. For using this TTM process, you offer a relevant theme with its prompting questions, making sure to give clear instructions on how to use the material and ask your client to go and write from whatever prompt is most useful (however you define that outcome).

Typically, the therapist does not choose the right prompt or questions to respond to. The client reads all the prompts and sees what gets stirred inside of them, either a gentle nudge or a tug of discomfort. That is the importance of having many diverse questions. This is client-centered, typically not therapist-managed or directed. The therapist offers the theme, not the question(s) to be answered. You, the therapist, might suggest/direct the person to look at three or four prompts that you would imagine will be most productive for that person. Generally, though, the work is most powerful, helpful, and effective when the client makes their own choice.

You might ask the person to read what they have written to someone in their world after asking for only supportive feedback. Alternatively, you may ask them not to read it to anyone else until they have read it to you, and together you decide what would be the better way to go forward with their careful words. You might ask your client to write on the same subject one, two, or three times to see where they go with it.

EXAMPLE

Jane, a high-powered, brilliant, accountant, and a fantastic person had accolades and successes that would impress anyone. You would experience her strength, insight, and talent if you met her. Like so often in high tech, one day you are the hero, and the next, you are the villain. Jane's day came, as most do, seemingly out of nowhere. She was blindsided when her peer manager told her she thought it was time for her to look for another job.

Yikes. Jane was in shock. She was referred for therapy to help her stay upright. She was completely destabilized and frozen. We all know that when someone is in horrible pain, doing work in therapy can be complicated. Of course, therapy is usually only a limited time in one's week, as was true for Jane. One hour a week, or even two, would never move her to the healing she desperately and understandably needed.

TTM to the rescue. Jane was offered the theme of "Having a big life or a small life." She took the questions/prompts home and could only read them the first week. She could not bring herself to write anything.

> *But, her healing self, her self-care self, rather than her devastated self, allowed her inner wisdom to begin to perk inside.*

She found two questions that she felt compelled to answer and did. She brought them into therapy and read them to her therapist; she had done some profound, meaningful, deeply valuable probing and searching to find what was ahead for her. The TTM process moved her along, on her own and in therapy, where her inner wisdom of what to write about took her on a path to see more about who she was now. This process sped up her awareness, choices, and capacity to self-reflect and gave her and her therapist a way to use their time together in an enhanced and productive way. Jane decided to take four months to heal, clean her house, exercise more, and use the TTM process to find her way in the world after the trauma of being forced out of her big job.

Part Two:
UNCOVERING TREASURES THAT MATTER IN PRACTICE: HOW TO USE TTM IN YOUR WORK

UNCOVERING TREASURES THAT MATTER, IN PRACTICE

As therapists, we always look for the best way to help our clients. TTM can be adapted to every possible therapy setting and configuration – individual therapy, couples therapy, workshops, groups – if it speaks to you. The themes and prompts, the juicy part of this approach, are provided to you and are available to your client without revision – unless, of course, you determine that changing something else is relevant or better – you have a seasoned therapist providing you with material that has taken years to create.

INDIVIDUAL THERAPY

Our work with individuals, a primary part of therapists' daily life, has many variations and options for how to make a difference with and for our clients. The TTM method is a meaningful and in-depth addition to your possibilities, your toolbox.

> **Less a technique and more a process in which your client can engage in between sessions or when you sit together.**

So often, someone will say to me, and I imagine to you, something that you know is a significant statement of how they see themselves and how they show up in the world. Much of the TTM method has come from those blazing, exquisitely clear insights that clients have shared with me.

A FEW EXAMPLES OF TTM WITH INDIVIDUAL CLIENTS

Just this past week, two different people said almost the exact words in describing their painful way of relating to the people around them. Lilly, an event planner, has been struggling with finding her voice with her husband of 30 years. She sees disapproval in his face anytime she imagines or he does not agree with something she has on her mind. Her strategy over many years has been to acquiesce with resentment, accommodate, withdraw to "keep the peace," or turn herself into a pretzel to keep everything steady.

Finally, some months ago, she had had it and burst forth with years of accumulated anger, hurt, dismay, and distrust of whether her husband even liked her. Of course, this pleaser style is ever present in many people and, indeed, in our clients, and may be valid for us, the therapist, being too nice.

Perhaps some of us are "recovering nice people," having learned that we need to say what is true to keep the kind of relationships we value and want to stay in.

Lilly's outburst did not solve the pain she was experiencing, but it led to a talk about going forward in a more productive and satisfying way. Easier said than done. A theme I frequently offer my clients is— "Finding your voice." Some people may think of that as wearing a mask vs. allowing themselves to be seen. Depending on the person and their situation, I offer a theme that seems most useful, ask them to read the questions, and see what stirs feelings in them. Then I request they go home and write what they need to say about that question or others, not literal answers to any questions but a narrative about what comes up inside them. As most of us have experienced, not all clients do homework for all sorts of reasons. Because the value of the TTM method is in writing, reading, and being supported (that is the evidence-based protocol), encouraging/nudging/even offering a space in the office to do that writing is all part of what is possible. How you, the therapist, choose to use this method is up to you. If your client will not write, the valuable, although a second-best option, is to invite that person to talk about what question(s) are important to them. Sometimes, after that discussion, the writing request becomes more possible;

once the person has seen the value in focusing on and addressing the probing prompts, they are more curious and motivated to write.

Using the TTM method with Jane, a scientist, was significant and helpful. Jane had extensive trauma in her history and lived a mostly isolated life. Even though she works and had recently started to work out, she could not connect with her peers. Jane froze at the idea of showing up with another face-to-face.

She said, "If I'm seen, something bad can happen," as it had many times in her past. Offering her the words "wearing a mask vs. being seen" resonated with her view of how she has been and is in the world. Just the words helped her see herself more clearly. Then, after several encouraging talks, she began to write, write, and write and read what she had felt, seen, and done. This revealing set of stories became the basis for our clinical work over the next six months and was pivotal in her being able to see herself and the world in which she lives freshly. She saw it. We saw it together. She wrote and rewrote, read, and reread her stories to me weekly, among the other things we talked about during this time. Jane, at nearly 50, had never even thought of many of the stories she now was writing about weekly. While some ideas were new to her, others she had recalled but not had a context to put them in for herself. She had felt so damaged that a few hours of therapy a week would have taken forever to uncover all that the stories revealed. With this profoundly connecting work that she was willing to do on her own, the therapy hours were more productive, healing, and valuable.

Zane, a CEO and my client from many years ago returned to therapy as his life, he said, was "falling apart." His business was failing, and, at that moment, his wife decided she wanted to be in a relationship with a woman, not him. He was in agony. He was in a crisis. At first, therapy was about helping him manage his shock and pain. After six weeks, since he was a head-centered person who valued treatment enough to come and ask for help, he was still most comfortable when he had things to figure out, learn what had happened, and how to go forward. He needed support, insight, and focus because he was adrift and painfully uncomfortable. Writing became part of how he coped, learned, explored, and sorted out what had happened. For a long time, he wrote from the theme, "Lightness and Darkness," finding many prompts that spoke to him. On multiple occasions, he wrote on the same topic/question because more and more kept emerging for him. The idea that there is light and dark in every life, permanence, and impermanence in every life was affirming and anchoring for him. He wrote. He read. He wrote. He read. He found clarity and insights in writing and the discussions we had. Indeed, any skilled therapist might have asked their client to write about how they experienced things if that was any part of the therapy, they thought could be valuable. However, these specific prompts gave Zane a direction, a central organizing viewpoint on which to anchor his thoughts, feelings, sensations, and experiences. For him, there was solace in seeing the universal theme and being reassured that he was not the only person in the world who had suffered such loss. He had targeted ideas, prompts, and themes to explore to help him personally.

> **In talking to one of my esteemed colleagues just now, he reminded me that he used these themes and prompts for clients who do not seem able or willing to bring questions, observations, feelings, thoughts, and insights into the therapy room.**

He frequently looks at the list and wonders if this or that one might provoke a meaningful discussion. Not all therapists would feel the wish, desire, or even think it relevant or appropriate to initiate such a discussion. For those of us who would and do, we know it works.

EXAMPLE

Jim felt terrible that his wife, Jennie, was so lonely. Inside, Jim, that sweet guy everyone liked, was a terrified person. His worth was tied up in making money. He had the horrible dilemma of providing money, what he defined as his only value, or being a more available partner, something he was not exceptionally skilled at doing. Jim's father, his model of how a man should be with his family, was gone most of the time, traveling to make money and, as it turned out, having many affairs. Jim did not want Jennie to think poorly about his father, so while Jennie knew his parents were divorced, and there had been lots of fighting, his father did provide money for the family. Jim had the pieces, the information, about how his Father had been, but he had not been able to put together his own story of what he thought it meant to be a man, to be a Father. It all seemed so obvious when he wrote the story that the only value he thought his father brought to the family was money, and he was doing the same thing. While this awareness did not change everything immediately, it gave Jim a new look at what he was doing and why. Sure, in therapy, this story might have emerged. With TTM, however, the question prompted Jim to write about and tell his story to make the discovery and connection totally apparent and helpful quickly and cleanly.

COUPLES THERAPY

We are beyond fortunate to be at a time and place when working with couples is supported by outstanding research, extensive information on how to assist couples with their concerns about communication, deep betrayal, and everything in between; workshops, seminars, training sequences, and consultation from genuinely innovative and brilliant therapists are all available resources. A missing support is how to help couples interact with their writing experience and share it with the most important person in their lives. TTM offers unique and page-turning ideas that can be used in parallel, independently, or as adjuncts to other couples' work.

As with any client, we look to say and offer ideas, insights, awareness, or other interventions that will make a difference will be helpful. We often can and do find what needs to be provided from our extensive background as a clinician. However, writing has seldom been suggested as a method to help each person in the couple find their voice, tell their story, and recover their inner wisdom in an accessible way. As is true when working with an individual, each person in a couple has stories to tell. Often couples' work can get bogged down with whose version of what happened is significant and accurate. Clients will say, "If we cannot agree on what happened, how can we figure out what to do about it?" That is an all too frequent roadblock, possibly resistance, vulnerability, or inner chaos, but it can be bypassed when asking each person to write their story about what happened, what gets stirred for them, and how that impacts them. Let me make this clearer.

Meet Beth and George. Each said they genuinely wanted to be together but got derailed almost daily. The battleground was over crumbs on the counter. Yes, crumbs on the counter. Don't write them off, as some people might. Many of us in relationships have our version of crumbs on the counter. Stay with me here, please. They were so ingenious in figuring this out that even the most imaginative therapist might have taken a long time to understand. Every time they talked about those crumbs, the pain was more profound, and the threats, spoken or not, got more dire. They did it, though. They figured it out when each was asked to write about "crumbs on the counter" rather than talk about it again. This is what emerged.

Beth, an artist, is an outstanding and creative cook. She likes to make pasta from scratch and sauces with real vegetables. She attends to their health needs and makes luscious food from her long line of Italian teachers. She talked about how much love and energy she puts into the food she makes and how much she hopes and wants the food to please George. All their friends enjoy invitations to their expansive table of the best food you can imagine.

George, an engineer, is a loving and kind person. When Beth cooks, it is George's job to clean up. Beth admits she is a messy cook. Both agree that George does a great job cleaning up, except he frequently leaves a pot to soak and rarely wipes down the counters, leaving crumbs on the counter. Since both Beth and George work, they are often tired by the end of the day. Beth acknowledged that when she is tired after work, she might go on a "crumb hunt." That is, she might go looking for trouble and see if George has genuinely cleaned up before she sets up to make another fantastic meal for them alone or their company. George, while highly motivated to be a good partner, said he wants to do the right thing; he sometimes thinks he did what was required or did not need to do more. As they read their stories to each other, there was nodding and validation that what each person was saying was accurate. Already this was better than the triggering experiences that each had been discussing. To reach a place of agreement through writing, rather than experiencing the more acrimonious interactions they had been having, was already healing. And there was more. As Beth and George had their private time to write their telling and clarifying stories, something meaningful and helpful happened. Each described their core pain, personal wounds, and how that history played out in their repetitive fight. Each of them felt compassion for the other and could also see their disappointment and distress at what felt like a re-enactment of what they had grown up experiencing. On their own, they made the connection from the past to the present. All this healing occurred through writing their story. They had used the theme and the prompts about the rules in their families and how they each imagined, expected, and hoped the other would "behave" or be in their relationship.

EXAMPLE

Paul and John, married for two years, had been in couples therapy for about six months. Paul, a physician, and John, a design professor, had each been married before and came to their relationship with definite ideas about how things should go and who should do what. Each was committed to their relationship and ensuring things were "fair" between them. Defining "fair" became a focal point of our work, the operative factor in how this relationship could work out over time. What equates with what? Did "doing the laundry" means gathering, washing, drying, folding, and putting away all the clothes? If one person cooked four nights a week, who would pay for the meals they ate out? Did the floor need to be swept each day to collect all the dog hairs, or was once a week sufficient? Was cooking a meal equivalent to bringing home take-out? Their beloved dog, Alfred, needed many walks; was it "fair" if one person's walk was shorter than the other? And on and on and on. If John wanted the table set with placemats, napkins, and even candles and Paul didn't care about any of that, feeling fine about eating while standing at the stove, how could those different needs be clarified as "fair" or not? A seemingly endless series of discussions ensued because there are a zillion ways chores, responsibilities, and lifestyles can be defined. The efforts to problem solve they had tried before were totally frustrating because, as two brilliant people, there was always a nuance, a distinction, something that made this situation distinct in its way. They wanted all this to be easier because being together was deep and sweet for each of them.

Any therapist would want to help these engaging, brilliant, dear people. A range of therapists had helped each of them in the past dealing with their previous relationships and lives, and one other therapist had tried to help with this "fairness" struggle. What helped was having each of them write on the theme, "Rules of Your Life"; the latest and greatest, the old standbys, and what is right and good now. They each made rather endless lists of the rules they had inside of them (and most of us have very long lists) and then reviewed them to see what was helpful, productive, and significant. After the first round of looking at rules was complete, instead of trying to figure out each and every situation to debate what might be "fair endlessly," they created a joint roadmap of the rules to bring into this relationship.

Of course, there was a power struggle here, a struggle that could be addressed from a variety of therapeutic styles. Many of those approaches may have been helpful. What is particularly salient here is that the theme, "Rules of Your Life," is a concept that most of us carry around inside us. If we can own the rules we hold dear and see the ones we can let go of, we have a tool in our relationships that can be used in many situations.

The TTM method shifted the clinical work from the interaction between Paul and John and invited them to look at their individual contributions to their difficulties. Then they came back together with new insight and a deeper understanding of who they are and how they can become a part of the necessary adaptation in their relationship. This could sound or seem like a cognitive exercise; instead, it is a profoundly evocative process of self-searching and self-discovery.

Just the notion that writing one's story and reading it to one's partner can get to the deeper connections within each person may seem simple. However, not many therapists offer this idea to their clients and have the theme and questions, the focus, to help their clients do just that. Healing happens when clients find their own expression, wisdom, and clarity.

As is true with individuals, groups, or workshops, couples who are offered the opportunity to write their stories have the distinct and idiosyncratic possibility of connecting with each other through their inner storyteller. This is a new way for them to gain the therapeutic experience possible through the TTM writing method.

WORKSHOPS

Depending on your education/training, supervision, and experience, offering a workshop may require additional help. Here is the step-by-step on how to run these workshops. You must assess your scope of competence to provide a workshop or seek supervision and help from a more experienced person.

I know they all work after running many workshops and hundreds of sessions. Your clinical practice, the why and how of what you do, can be adapted, and adjusted to suit your time, talents, and desires. And they all work. Yes, of course, in any workshop, there can be and often is at least one person with some additional needs that must be addressed. We tell you what we have learned to assist you in managing and helping the group be safe and productive. That help from us does not replace the training, skill, and supervision you have received. Be sure to get what you need to be ethical, that is, to practice within your scope of competence if you run workshops.

A WORKSHOP FORMAT

One day option, 4.5 hours

Imagine spending three, four, or five hours with a group of six to twelve people exploring a theme together. After multiple variations over years of offering these workshops, here is the option that participants and I like the best. And, of course, it can and will work with many variations, adding or subtracting what you want to do, what audience you serve, your clinical orientation, expertise, and experience.

STEP-BY-STEP GUIDE

Send the introductory narrative, the theme you have chosen as the focus of the workshop, and the prompting questions to each participant seven to ten days before the day of the workshop. The instructions on what you ask people to do are critical. Reminding the participants they can address the theme in a light, even superficial, top-down view or a profoundly probing, carefully considered way, which may stir discomfort, or anything in between will be yours to suggest or determine. If this is therapy, you may want to offer a range and see what people bring. Since whatever someone shows up with tells us about who they are and where they are in their lives, taking note of how they address the theme will be clarifying to you, the therapist, and the client, too. Of course, offering the client a range of ways to address the writing gives them more choices, which is always a good thing.

NOON: THE WORKSHOP STARTS

Tell them. Be on Time for The Workshop. You Are Welcome to Arrive Up To 15 Minutes before the workshop starts. To be respectful of the people who come on time, I always start the workshop at the time promised. I allow people to arrive early so they can settle in. If they come late, I do not return to the workshop's beginning. I fill any latecomer in when we have a break. I make sure to tell participants that I plan to start on time.

THE PHYSICAL SPACE

Make sure all the elements of the physical space are carefully considered, including— enough light, no background noise, big enough chairs for people of all sizes and physical needs, temperature, etc. This Is essential. If someone is uncomfortable, the energy in the room is impacted.

NOON TO 12:30 PM

Settle in. Discuss the theme of the day (they received the written introduction and prompts ahead of time.)

Introduce the topic with either the short narrative presented in the written material before each theme, your thoughts, or simply ask the participants what came up for them when they started to address the theme.

- Allow time for each person to speak, but do not require people to participate.
- Brief breathing exercise

After the discussion, do a brief breathing exercise or guided meditation related to the workshop's theme. Send the participants off with an open-ended thought or image to help them explore the theme within themselves during the next phase of the workshop.

12:30 PM TO 2 PM

During this time, participants may write, revise, or edit what they wrote about the theme before coming to the workshop, make collages, ponder, and meditate.

LUNCH OR A SIMPLE SNACK AND DRINKS ARE OFFERED*

During these 90 minutes, participants may write for the first time—even though they had the questions for 7-10 days, revise what they have written, make a collage—with supplies you either asked them to bring or have provided, ponder, meditate or whatever they need to do to take care of themselves. Make sure there are quiet spaces to sit and places where participants can interact.

*Offering lunch or snacks provides warmth and intimacy that some therapists will see as deepening the sense of community over shared food; others will say it is inappropriate. For me, offering food to share (simple or elaborate) sets a tone that invites the connections I want to foster.

2 PM TO 4 PM

- Reading, storytelling, and sharing with supportive comments offered from participants and the therapist.
- Make sure there is time for everyone. Watch the clock. Try to keep it fair, so each person gets about the same amount of time for reading and getting feedback.

Ask each participant if they would like someone to take notes about what other people say so they can just listen and not try to remember what each member of the workshop says. If they want a scribe, ask for a volunteer.

As a therapist, one question to ask and answer for yourself is if you want to push the participants to move beyond what their writing brings to them. Do you want to add probing questions or thoughts for them to take with them? I typically do that if the person is receptive to that deepening possibility.

If someone has not written, let them talk about the theme within their time limit. If someone does not wish to read or talk about the theme, allow that to be okay. If someone has found something unrelated to the theme that has emerged for them, either ask them to go last to talk about what has come up or let them take a turn when they are ready; the latter is my preferred response. In therapy, the psyche brings us what we need to consider when it does.

4-4:30 PM
WRAP UP

Ask each person to write a few notes of what they want to take away from the workshop for themselves, from their reading and getting feedback, or from what they heard and experienced from the other people. Then ask for concluding comments and appreciation.

4:30 PM
GOODBYES

An example of a workshop that shook the earth for each of us.

The theme was about health. Each person had a meaningful and poignant story to tell. There was the cancer diagnosis, the six miscarriages, and the fears and the worries. And then Susan read her story. Susan's family had too many people with Alzheimer's disease, too many to list, she said. She was "walking worried" about her own medical situation. She decided to write a letter to her husband and grown children about what she would want if she got Alzheimer's disease, how they could show her love, what she felt she would need, and what would make her more comfortable even if she could not tell them at the time.

As someone who mostly did not ask for what she wanted in life, just that she was willing, able, interested, motivated, and desired to say what was important to her was breathtaking, and then she read her letter. The bright and sunny room filled with the light she envisioned, filled with her treasured art supplies, a place where her beloved doggie could roam and be in bed with her, close to where the people she loves live, and where she could be appreciated for the woman, she had been, were all expressed in exquisite language.

With tears flowing from most of us, she read about her plans to read the letter to her husband, her grown sons, and her dearest friend. Just the idea of writing this letter, and its value, became a gift to each of us as we considered what we might want to say and do for our own future lives—the gift of a lifetime.

GROUPS

As pioneered by Irvin Yalom, MD, group work's power comes from receiving feedback from others (Yalom, 1995). In a TTM group, only supportive feedback and compassion are allowed. As with other group methods, participants can learn, grow, consider, and see themselves in ways not as available individually, just by the nature of more people seeing, saying, sharing, connecting, supporting, and responding – an experience rarely possible in daily life (Brown, 2018).

Dr. James Birren, the creator of the Guided Autobiography method, always pointed out that his method is "therapeutic, but not therapy." (Birren & Cochran, 2001). While participants are specifically told to refrain from sharing negative judgments of others in these groups, what individuals may experience within themselves is still enlightening. The gift of therapeutic growth comes from being with different people, even in modest ways, and learning to see our own lives in new, perhaps revised ways.

Groups are effective because we learn about ourselves from hearing the stories of others.

> **Since knowing what we do not know about ourselves is challenging, it helps to hear how another person sees and handles what life has brought and to receive supportive feedback. In addition, a meaningful way to learn about ourselves is in the judgments we make of others, both positive and negative. What someone else does or does not do, says, or does not say, may provoke an emotional response that can help us see an unknown, denied, or underdeveloped part of ourselves.**

Are you ready for group work? Some of you may believe you lack the skills to be a group leader. Only you know what your past training in group work has been. Most therapists have some education in group work. You may have taken a course in group therapy in graduate school. Or perhaps, like many therapists, you were required to participate in a group experience during your training. For some, that was enlightening; for others, it was torture, disliked both for the requirement and what took place in the group. This book clarifies that offering groups of the type we are suggesting is quite distinct from those training experiences. Whether or not you have direct experience running groups, the material included in this workbook will give you all the content you need to facilitate a group.

Another option. A sequence of groups.

GETTING STARTED

The therapist first needs to gather participants for the TTM group. See the appendix for finding participants. Six to eight members are good; that allows each person time to share their stories, be heard, seen, and supported in the small group. You will set the schedule for the total number of sessions to meet. A group with five to ten sessions gives everyone the chance to make a connection to themselves and the other participants. You, the therapist, and the group leader guide the process of reflection on all the writing themes. Each session ends with a writing assignment guided by questions related to each week's theme. Participants bring two or three pages of their writing (written at home) to share at the next session. You teach them to give each other supportive, encouraging feedback. Gently redirect if critique, judgment, or intrusive challenging occurs.

WHAT'S INCLUDED IN EACH SESSION

Each group session includes themes and prompts focused on issues and problems that therapists regularly see in private practice.

For each session, you will need:

- A description of the week's theme.

- Materials and handouts

PROMPTING QUESTIONS FOR THE WEEK'S WRITING ASSIGNMENT

In your TTM group, you can use this material in several ways. You might ponder the week's topic in advance, then introduce the topic in your own words. You might read directly from the theme and prompts. Or you might simply announce the topic and let participants speak from their own experiences and perspectives, co-creating their introduction to the topic. The important thing is what is suitable for you. You will decide the number of sessions the group will meet and the specific issue the group will focus on. For example, if you choose that your first group will meet for five weeks and work on relationship issues, there are several themes you might select. Some suggestions:

Relationships: The Good, the Troubles, What Needs Attention

Giver and Taker: The Helper and Receiver; Good, Bad, Making Choices

Friendships: The Sweetness And The Pain

CONNECTIONS

For session one, your focus will be on building a group identity, explaining what the group process entails, setting up the ground rules, discussing feedback methods, going over confidentiality issues, and generally explaining step by step how the group works, what the expectations are for the members, and what benefits they can expect. Finally, the therapist will explain the TTM writing method and give them the theme and writing prompts for their homework assignment. The following week, they will bring in their two pages of writing on the relevant theme.

STEP-BY-STEP GUIDE: SESSION ONE

RELATIONSHIPS: WHAT DO YOU CELEBRATE?
WHAT TROUBLES YOU AND MIGHT NEED ATTENTION?

PROCESS

- Group members introduce themselves to each other.

- Discuss the structure and expectations for the group sessions.

- Provide an overview of the five group sessions.

- Read and discuss the Group Guidelines.

- Have group members read and sign the confidentiality form.

- Ice Breaker exercise.

- Introduce the first theme, a theme of your choosing.

MATERIALS/HANDOUTS (SEE APPENDIX)

Participant information form/informed consent

Confidentiality form.

Group Guidelines form

How to Give Feedback form

THEME ONE:

Relationships: What Do You Celebrate? What Troubles You and Might Need Attention?

INTRODUCTION AND WELCOME

Welcome everyone as they come in and ask them to complete the Participant Information form/informed consent and the Confidentiality form. This Participant information form is not to be shared with the group; keep it for your use. If someone wants to give their contact information to another group member, that is their choice.

Discuss the structure of the session, how the time will be used, when there will be a break and when the session will end. Understand that people may feel anxious about what will be expected of them, what they will write, and what they will share. Explain how the group process works and the therapeutic benefits that can occur from the group work. Here are some introductory comments that may help you.

"In this group, you will have the opportunity to consider four themes at whatever depth you choose. In deciding what to write about, reading it to the other group members, and receiving supportive, encouraging responses without criticisms or negative judgments, you will have the chance to learn what others hear about you and see what you may not have noticed about yourself before, and perhaps get a new idea, or thought, or path forward to consider."

AGREEMENTS: DISCUSS IN THE GROUP.

- *You must attend, be on time, and participate in all sessions.* If you will be late or cannot attend, let the leader know as soon as possible. If there is the time at the next session, you may be able to read your story then. Or you may be able to schedule a time to read your story with the leader.

- *Be respectful of other group members.* No crosstalk, judgmental comments or behaviors, criticism, interruptions, leaving during a story (except in a true emergency), distracting behavior, or talking to other group members when people are reading their stories.

- *Confidentiality.* This is critical. While you, the leader, cannot guarantee what the group members reveal outside the group, ask each member to verbally agree to keep private what they hear in the group, the name of the participants, and anything about their stories. While the group member may talk about their experience of what was shared, be extremely careful never to disclose information that may reveal to the other group members directly or indirectly.

- *Some stories may be uncomfortable for you to hear. Listen quietly.* Take care of yourself but do not attempt to stop someone else from reading their story. Everyone's stories need to be told. You can leave if you feel you must before the discussion of the story but not during the reading of it.

TTM WRITING

Next, it is time to talk about the writing assignments expected of each group member. Explain that expressive writing is writing from within without focusing on spelling and grammar. You might say, "This is writing from your emotional self.

> **When you start to write your story, your inner critic may show up and give you a hard time about writing at all and about writing what is important, what is true for you to write. Think about that critic as a *protector* who is there to help you in your life.**

Sometimes that critic is mean, and sometimes that critic brings you important things to consider. That critic may even bring up what you most need to write about and consider." Ask the group members to write as if they were telling a story to a trusted friend. This is similar to yet different from journal writing. You can say to them, "When keeping a journal, generally no one else reads it, and maybe you don't either. With this method, you will write on your own, uncensored, and then read it in class with your small group of supportive listeners. You will grow through your writing, from being seen and heard to the feedback and comments given by the people in the group. When it comes to reading in the group, be sure only to read what you are okay with sharing. Sometimes, even if you write something to be shared, you may not be comfortable doing so when the time comes to read." Ask, again, even though everyone has agreed already, that everyone keep what they hear confidential. And, of course, that cannot be guaranteed. Advise them also to "be sure to take care of yourself and read what you are okay to read."

FREE WRITING EXERCISE

Ask each person in the group to take out a pen and paper. Have them consider what relationships mean to them. "What do you honestly think and feel about your current relationships? Spend five minutes free writing on this topic." When the time is up, ask each person to read what they have written, if willing. Discuss what comes up.

If someone does not want to read everything they have written, do not force them. Ask them to read a portion. Talk to them afterward and discern if that is situational or if declining to read will become an ongoing issue. If this is a one-time concern, then no problem. If you, the group leader, believe this will be an ongoing concern, the person may not be suitable for the group. Of course, this will be a challenging situation. Get consultation on what to do if that would help you make a good decision and communicate it in a non-blaming, non-shaming way.

HOW THIS GROUP WORKS

What is group therapy? How does it work? How is it different from individual therapy? How is it still therapy? These are all topics for discussion and will set the tone for your group. Included in this section is the importance of confidentiality and trust.

First, refer to the Agreements discussed at the beginning of the session: attend all sessions, be on time, honor confidentiality, complete the written assignments, and give supportive feedback. Discuss this again and make sure everyone understands and agrees.

The benefits of group therapy, Instead of relating to one person, a therapist, you are fortunate to get responses from your group members, people you will get to know during the weekly meetings. You hear from many people about what they hear and receive their supportive and encouraging responses to what you read. In these groups, by design and direction, there are no criticisms, judgments, or challenges to what you said or did; you can continue to explore within yourself.

This process can relieve and heal what has happened in your life. First, you get a chance to review what you remember. You write about those memories and then take another look at the feelings, thoughts, emotional reactions, and beliefs you have carried with you about the experience described in the story. After you share your story in the group, you will hear supportive comments on how other people receive and respond to your story. Finally, you get to review the additional self-reflection, ideas, and impressions from the other people. That is a way to relieve and heal what you have experienced, and that is therapy. That is therapeutic.

FEEDBACK: DISCUSS WITH THE GROUP MEMBERS

All relevant forms are provided in the Appendices. Hand out the form on feedback and go over it in the session, so everyone clearly understands how to give positive, supportive feedback to one another.

INTRODUCE AND HAND OUT THEME ONE
RELATIONSHIPS: THE GOOD, THE TROUBLES, WHAT NEEDS ATTENTION

Please read the introduction and discuss relationships with the group to get them thinking and talking about their feelings. Let them review the specific questions offered on their own so they can have their own experience with them.

Most of us want personal relationships. Few among us prefer to be alone. Being close to other people is a deep need, so profound that most of us cannot live without being involved with others. And yet, close relationships are complicated. Think about your hopes and dreams for your connection with others. Notice where you have fulfilled those wishes and where ongoing or new desires and longings exist. Rarely is there someone who says that they are content, all the time, with the quality, depth, and range of the connections they have? What do you celebrate? Whom do you honor? Do they know? Do they know what doesn't work for you? What troubles you and might need or does need attention? What is there to do to have close/closer relationships?

SENSITIZING QUESTIONS AND PROMPTS

1. What is a good relationship? Do you have a good relationship(s) with anyone, someone? How do you know? What do the people around you say to you about your relationship with them? What do you tell yourself about the relationships you have — be they family, friends, romantic, casual, intense, hoped for, whatever kind?

2. Do you define yourself by the relationships you have, have, wish you had, or never had?

3. Being with your authentic self, without hesitating or shying away from complete immersion in your total pleasure and joy, what parts/moments/aspects do you celebrate about the people you know? With that same forthright, unflinching look, what troubles you in your friendships, family, romance, with children, including the absence of any of those kinds of relationships?

4. Many say their relationship, particularly a primary one, is "good enough." When does that become settling? Is it okay to settle?

5. If you have relationships that satisfy you, what defines them? If you are looking for a satisfying personal relationship, how do you imagine your life would be if you had what you think you want?

6. What do you do, not do, that enhances the relationships you seek or have? What do you do or not do that interferes with your having the relationship(s) you desire? If you asked people you trust what they see as your way of making relationships go well, what would they tell you? If you asked those same people how you get in your way, what might they say, especially if they were not worried about hurting you?

7. If you were going to do a relationship inventory of what good things you bring to a primary/romantic relationship, friendship, family connection, and what things you do that are complicated, problematic, annoying, or worrisome, what would be on those lists? If you choose not to write about this question, you might ask yourself why.

8. What are three things you could do today that would expand the possibility of your having a new, close, personal, deep relationship if that is something you want? What are three things you could do, beginning today, to create or improve your relationship, even if they are already good?

9. What can you celebrate that you do or don't do that makes you a fantastic partner/friend/family member? What can you celebrate that the other person/people do or don't do that makes that person a tremendous partner?

10. Let's get real. Are you the kind of partner you would like to have? How so? Let's get real. Is your partner the kind of partner who is good and right for you?

11. You want to meet someone. How do you assess that they are good for you?

12. You are with someone in romance or friendship. How do you assess that you are bringing your best self to the relationship? How do you evaluate that partner is bringing their best self to the relationship?

13. One behavior that many partners demonstrate is called summarizing self-syndrome. They keep telling their partner what the partner needs to do. The partner does not do it. This goes on for years. What are alternatives besides continuing to educate the other person on how they need to be?

14. One behavior that many single people who want to be in a relationship do is doing the same thing over and over to meet and develop relationships. Think about someone who was where you are and now is with someone. Besides luck, what did they do that could inform your choices?

15. What is your dream for a relationship? Do you have that relationship? Do you bring it? Now what?

SUMMING UP

Go over the assignment for the first class. Everyone should understand the purpose and guidelines for the group. Also, remind them they will write two pages, in a stream of conscious way or go with the flow, on one of the questions, and be prepared to read it during the second half of the group the following week. Make sure each person has your contact information and knows how to get in touch with you if they have questions before the next session.

Ask everyone to say how they feel and list one takeaway from the first session.

After you've taken your group through the sessions, you may evaluate the experience to deepen your group leader skills. Once you offer your first group, we predict you'll find it so satisfying that it won't be long before you plan and recruit for additional groups.

EXAMPLE FROM A GROUP SESSION

Allie and her Mother. Mothers. Mothers. Mothers. Most everyone has stories about their Mother.

Allie was the last to read her story on a bright and sunny California Saturday morning. The first thing she said before pulling out the multiple handwritten pages with paragraph after paragraph scratched out was that her family rule was, "keep the family business in the family." Still, at 73, she was determined to try another way. Allie was frequently the quietest person in the group, not so much shy as hesitant, friendly, and impersonal. Here is her story.

"I think I love my Mother. I always thought I loved my Mother. I do love my Mother. And she drives me crazy. She calls me up and tells me when she is coming to see me and how long she will stay. She had me when she was 17. Now, at 90, fortunately, she still lives alone, drives, and does what she wants. When she comes to see me, she has A LOT to say about everything, including what I do and don't do. She rearranges the kitchen and laundry cabinets without asking, gathers things she thinks I should recycle, talks incessantly, and insists on cooking, cooking, and cooking, even though I do not want to eat the food she makes. I cannot say no to her coming or staying or telling me how she feels I need to live my life. Here I am at this age, and I feel like I am the 13-year-old being told to clean my room.

I think I love my Mother. I always thought I loved my Mother. I do love my Mother. Those words go through my head a thousand times a day when I know she is coming when she is visiting and when I have talked to therapists about why I cannot say whatever I want to her—like that is not a good time to come, stay for three days instead of ten, or can we talk about what would be better for me. I cannot bring myself to say those words. I want to. I can't.

To the people around us, my Mother is cool. She drives. She cooks. She helps. She knows about current events. I cannot tell anyone what it is like for me."

Allie went on to say all the things she had tried to move her relationship with her Mother to a better place. She was keenly aware that even though her Mother was robust and independent, that could and would change sooner rather than later. She was so conflicted. Allie had written letters to her, not to send, about what she wanted to say, what she thought she should say. Her therapist had made many suggestions about how to help Allie find and express her needs and wishes. She just could not bring herself to say anything. She just couldn't. Her anguish was clear.

Allie read more and more of what she had written. When she was finished, there were 15 pages of mostly not read, scratched-out pages on the table in front of her.

There was quiet.

One group member said, "I understand." Another said, "That sounds so hard." A third person, Alice, said, "I know, I am like that with my kid. Oh my god. I am like that with my kid. Thank you for letting me see how that is for you." And a fourth person said, "I lost years and years and years with my Mother because I never told her anything about me. I was sure she would be hurt or not care or deny what I was saying."

Allie had broken the code of silence. She said out loud the unspeakable. Everything in the family was not as it looked or how it seemed to others.

Alice, the group member who acknowledged she was like Allie's Mother, implored Allie to tell her Mother what she had just read to the group. She said it was a gift. She offered to come and be there when she did. She said words that might make it easier for Allie's Mother to hear.

There was serendipity that day when Allie read her story, and Alice was there to speak about her experience. The good fortune of this kind happens frequently. Or something else occurs that is empowering, supportive, clarifying, and valuable.

Therapists want to help. Creating an environment where people can show up for each other when talking about real things, with a real person, with real feelings happens in these TTM groups. What power to hear someone say, I am like that problem person in your life, and this is what would be helpful so I could hear you better. Even if those words do not work, any of us would feel less alone with the choice.

Groups offer the chance to learn from others. In a TTM experience, with the focus on being helpful and supportive, not critical as – in telling Allie what she should do – there is a chance for healing, forward movement, and change. Telling your true story to people who want to know you is powerful.

Part Three:
METHOD

Ten Categories

Fifty Themes

Sensitizing Questions And Prompts

TEN CATEGORIES

CATEGORY I
GATHERING HISTORY: THE START OF SOMETHING NEW

THEMES

Childhood: A New Life Begins

Home: Where is It? What is it? The Real, the Hope, the Wish

Family: Who Was and Is Your Family?

Work and Career

Purpose in Your Life

The Meaning of Money

Acquiring Money

Talents: The Old, Forgotten, Wished For and the New and Yet to Be

CATEGORY II
THE CORE OF YOU

THEMES

Your Inner Selves

Inner Critic

Giver and Taker/ Helper and Receiver. Good, Bad, Making Choices

Feminine and Masculine. Masculine and Feminine. Gender Fluidity

CATEGORY III
CHOICE POINTS

THEMES

Where Have You Been in Your Life?

Pivotal Moments and Their Meaning

How will you remember? Your Belief, Filter, Definition of Who You Are

Gifts: Giving, Receiving, Tangible, Intangible

CATEGORY IV
RELATIONSHIPS

THEMES

Relationships: The Good, The Troubles, What Needs Attention

Children and Pets

Connections

Friendships: The Sweetness and The Pain

Personal Boundaries: Where, When, and How to Draw the Line

Heroes or Heroines and Villains

Romance: Who Were/Are They, Those Romantic People in Your Life

CATEGORY V
HEALTH AND WELL-BEING

THEMES

Physical Health

Your Body – Your Sexual Self

Your Mental Health

CATEGORY VI
TRANSITIONS

THEMES

Living Alone

Limits. Loss

Grief

CATEGORY VII
CONTEMPLATING

THEMES

Finding Your Voice

Triggers

Being Old. Being Young

Lightness and Darkness in Every Life

Softening Up or Toughening Up

Walking the Spiritual Path

CATEGORY VIII
DISCERNING

THEMES

Big Life. Little Life

Independence. Dependence. Are You Invested In One and Need To Find The Other?

Permanence. Impermanence

Risks Taken. Risks Not Taken

Rules of Your Life: The Latest and Greatest, The Old Standbys, What Is Right?

Truth and Fiction: What Is True In Your Life? What Is Fiction? What Is Clear? What Is Distorted?

Waking Up To … Letting Go Of …

CATEGORY IX
CELEBRATING

THEMES

Firsts. Lasts. Holidays and Other Occasions

Happy Birthday: The Real, The Remembered, The Hoped For

Uncovering Treasures That Matter: A Thing. A Person. An Experience

CATEGORY X
WHAT IS AHEAD? WHERE TO?

THEMES

Legacy: Legacy Letter, Who Are You, and What Do You Value? The Toasts You Want To Hear

If Not Now, When?

What I Know To Be So

Where Are You Going in Your Life and How Will You Get There?

What Matters? Now What?

CATEGORY I

GATHERING HISTORY: THE START OF SOMETHING NEW

Childhood: A New Life Begins

Home: Where is It? What is it? The Real, the Hope, the Wish

Family: Who Was and Is Your Family?

Work and Career

Purpose in Your Life

The Meaning of Money

Acquiring Money

Talents: The Old, Forgotten, Wished For and the New and Yet to Be

When we plan to move forward, starting something new is a helpful place to begin by looking back. By understanding where we've been and who we have become, we can start to move ahead in our life. As Soren Kierkegaard has said, "Life can only be understood backward; but it must be lived forwards." The very basics of who we are and from where we have come are indelible parts of us. While new experiences happen, our genetic makeup and core experiences become our story, our way of processing and collecting the knowledge of who we are. The themes and questions in this category direct your attention to your past: your childhood, the meaning of "home," your values, what money means in your worldview, talents, and more. Look at the surface recollections, dig further inside, or see what unexpectedly comes to your mind to access this elemental part of who you are. Examining these questions will uncover the important stories that define your life, where you came from, and what describes you as you reflect on your life.

CHILDHOOD: A NEW LIFE BEGINS

Childhood is the period of our lives when we are developing, attaching to others or not, learning, and becoming. This dramatic and powerful time of life is experienced in widely disparate ways. What happened then and who was a part of your life has meaning and consequences for the rest of your life. There are a zillion aspects of childhood. They all matter. Choosing what you consider the most important to recall, review, and explore is written about in many books.

Ask yourself each question offered. Consider responding to a question(s) that makes you smile, that you are attracted to answering, and to one or two you don't like or want to turn away from. Facing what you don't like, or are uncomfortable with, is often a path to the most significant learning. These questions are guides to prime or stimulate your memories and thoughts about your life. The questions are not intended to be answered in a literal manner. Read through each of them and react to the one(s) that open windows for you. Each life is unique, and the priming questions impact each of us differently.

SENSITIZING QUESTIONS AND PROMPTS

1. How do you describe your childhood? What worked? What didn't? Who was there? Who wasn't that should have been or might have been? How have those factors influenced and impacted your life?

2. In a few feeling words—including happy, sad, glad, mad, plus others—what are your primary feelings about your childhood? As you observe what you recall or notice, are you surprised, or is this the way you have thought about your childhood for years?

3. Most of us have some major stories that define our childhood. Whether you write a familiar story or not, list the main ideas captured in those stories. Good. Bad. Other.

4. Loss frequently occurs in childhood. For instance, a parent or caregiver becomes seriously ill or dies; a parent loses their job; the place where you lived became a problem in one way or another; your parent's divorce; a sibling appears with or develops a serious problem, physical or psychological. Did you experience childhood loss? What happened? As you think about the effect on you, what are some things that changed you in the short term or changed you for life forever?

5. Trauma and abuse are also a part of many people's childhood. Simply saying "yes" or "no" to the question if that was part of your life can be sufficient. Adding in more can be sufficient. Talking about the experience, the details, the help received, and the help needed can be sufficient. What is right for you?

6. Who were the important and positive people in your life—parents, caregivers, physicians, teachers, rabbis/ministers/priests, scout leaders, family friends, family members, and what did they bring to you?

7. Who were the important and negative people in your life—parents, caregivers, physicians, teachers, rabbis/ministers/priests, scout leaders, family friends, family members, and what did they bring to you?

8. If you had siblings, stepsiblings, or foster siblings, what experiences did you share, and how do those experiences impact your life?

9. If you were adopted, at what age did that happen? What is important to you about adoption?

10. What are the most joyful and celebratory times of your childhood? Are they related to achievements, experiences, travel, or others? What are the most difficult times of your childhood, and how come?

11. Is there one person, or more, who made a profound difference in your life, positive or negative? What is one story that captures something specific you have brought into your life now, positive, or negative, from that person? If they are still alive, is there something you want to say to them? If they have died, would you still want to write them a letter to express your feelings?

12. Are there some specific learning or "famous sayings" you have taken from the people who were part of your childhood life? What are they? As you take note of them and look at those messages, do they fit you now? Were they limiting or enhancing you during your childhood? Would you want to pass them on to your children if you have or will not have them?

13. In many children's lives, there is stretching or contorting to fit in. What stretching or contorting did you have to do, and how successful or poor were you at doing what was expected or required of you?

14. How were you labeled as a kid and by whom – a good kid, an athletic kid, an adventurous kid, a perfect kid, or a problem, as too much, highly sensitive, demanding, lazy, or what? How have those characterizations of you impacted your life?

15. Parental expectations for their child's life are often frequently discussed. What were you supposed to do and be? Be the physician like your Mom? Find an opposite sex partner, get married and have children? What did your parents expect of you? How has that gone if you did not fulfill their wishes, preferences, or needs?

16. Some people describe having a blissful and enriched childhood. Many people did not have such a childhood. What would you like to offer to your children?

HOME: WHERE IS IT? WHAT IS IT? THE REAL, THE HOPE, THE WISH

"Home, sweet home, be it ever so humble, there is no place like home." Home is where the heart is. Home is a retreat. Home is where you can put your feet up and leave your burdens behind. Where is home for you? What is home for you? Who needs to be there to be at home? Who should not be there to be at home? Home, the literal place, and the concept of home have profound meaning. Whether your literal home was peaceful or scary, idyllic, terrible, good, bad, or a combination at different times, we have images that transport us to what home is supposed to be, might be, or was. Home can be a physical location, a memory, a way of being – such as when you are in "flow" with your creative pursuits, a dream, a memory. Home can be safe or dangerous. It can have a comfortable sameness or be boring, be enlivening or deadening. Home can be steady or temporal. Home can be beautiful or not. Home can have the dishes done or the dishes stacked to the literal or figurative ceiling. Better is in the eyes of the beholder. Home can be quiet or noisy. All of these things can be good or not. Thinking about what home was and what home is, then and now, can help you gather those memories and create an intention for the home you desire.

Ask yourself each question offered. Consider responding to a question(s) that makes you smile, that you are attracted to answering, and to one or two you don't like or want to turn away from. Facing what you don't like, or are uncomfortable with, is often a path to the most significant learning. These questions are guides to prime or stimulate your memories and thoughts about your life. The questions are not intended to be answered in a literal manner. Read through each of them and react to the one(s) that open windows for you. Each life is unique, and the priming questions impact each of us differently.

SENSITIZING QUESTIONS AND PROMPTS

1. What does home mean to you? Who is there with you? What is there with you, e.g., a critter or two, a fireplace, a large window, a garden?

2. Is home where you grew up or where you live now; where you lived at a particular time; all the above or none of the above?

3. For some people, home is when they feel peace, create, or feel loved or safe. What feelings do you experience when you are "at home" or "happily at home"? How do you know you are not "at home" and not in a good place for you?

4. If the home is your "go-to" place in your mind and not particularly a location, where is it, e.g., in your imagination, when you are creating art/words/music/movement/ideas?

5. Does having friends and family there make a space a home?

6. Is home a good place, a bad place, or a combination? What makes that so?

7. Do you have or have you had the home you want? What made it so? What would that include or exclude if that is yet to be?

8. If you do not have the home you want, what would it take to make it what is just right for you? And who encourages those changes? What and who discourages those changes?

9. Do you have places in your home that express who you are and want to be? Where are they? If you don't, how come and can you make it so?

10. What comforts do you seek or have that make a place a home?

11. What small gestures or moments make you feel you are at home? e.g., a light that shines in the morning reminds me to breathe fully and know that I am at home, safe, where I want and need to be.

12. Many people endure — too much stuff, noise, and unsorted/unfinished work — so that home is less than it might be. Is that true for you? What steps would you take to have your home be what you want it to be? Or, how can you make a small vignette, a small space, where you can be "at home" meaningfully?

13. Do you invite people into your home? If so, how come? If not, is that okay?

14. Are there a few things you would always want with you, no matter where you are, to feel at home?

15. What was your best experience of being "at home"? When did you feel the most displaced, not at home? Is home a place, an experience, a feeling?

16. What makes home safe for you, if it ever is or has been? What makes home unsafe for you if it is ever unsafe?

17. If you went to the physical space where you live today and changed three things to make that place better for you, what would those things be?

18. What is a dream home for you?

Since home is a central organizing theme in our lives, here are deeper and more probing sensitizing questions in case you want or need to go further in your exploration, review, and healing.

1. In your mind, is it better to be alone and happy or with a person or people and unhappy?

2. How do you compromise too much to not be alone at home if you do? As you pause and think about that, are you making the right choice for yourself?

3. Many people are afraid, hesitant, and inexperienced at being alone, on their own, at home. If that is you, what could you imagine or create to change your attitude, so you are at choice about with whom to share your living space or sense of home?

4. What rooms within a building make where you live a home? For instance, having a place where the colors are just right, and they can surround you.

5. Can you have dust bunnies, a sink full of dirty dishes, an unmade bed, and whatever else that is undone and be comfortable at home? If yes, do you leave the dishes? If not, how come? Are there some ways of being that define "home" for you?

6. Whom do you invite into your home? Whom do you exclude? Do you decide or just let happen what happens? Do you make active or passive choices about this decision and other choices, too?

7. Sometimes, we know we should leave the place we live or the person we live with, the place we define as home. Is that true for you now? What are you going to do about that? Stay? Go? Think about it? Not think about it? Talk about it? Not talk about it? What do you feel about that choice?

8. If you are someone who frequently/mostly worries, frets, and is concerned, how does that impact the quality of life at home? What do you learn from acknowledging that way of being?

9. If you are someone who frequently/mostly looks at only the good, happy, and positive, are you letting yourself see the whole picture or denying some things that need attention?

10. In California and some other places, homes are expensive. What is the impact of that on you, if at all?

11. What must you do now? What changes are necessary to make home more of what you want and need it to be?

12. Is thinking about home good or not such a good thing to do? How come?

FAMILY: WHO WAS AND IS YOUR FAMILY

Our family histories include our families of origin (parents, grandparents, aunts, uncles, cousins, and more) and the families of our adult lives (spouses, partners, children, grandchildren, in-laws, plus others). Perhaps an adopted child, friend, or another person has been close to you and your family and has been important in your life; you may call them family members, too. Family can include a range of people. What were the origins and branches of your family? Did your family history have an impact on the direction your life took? Which family members were important in shaping your life, and how? Some people may have been important to you in positive ways and some in negative ways. Why did certain family members impact your life more than others?

Ask yourself each question offered. Consider responding to a question(s) that makes you smile, that you are attracted to answering, and to one or two you don't like or want to turn away from. Facing what you don't like, or are uncomfortable with, is often a path to the most significant learning. These questions are guides to prime or stimulate your memories and thoughts about your life. The questions are not intended to be answered in a literal manner. Read through each of them and react to the one(s) that open windows for you. Each life is unique, and the priming questions impact each of us differently.

SENSITIZING QUESTIONS AND PROMPTS

1. Whom do you consider to be your family? Why do they get that status or role?

2. Who held power in your family and made the major decisions? How do you know? What do you think about how that went?

3. What family members have you felt closest to, and which ones felt most distant? Why? Were there any family members who were or are your model of a good life or one to avoid?

4. Did you like your family and felt supported and loved? Or not? What impacts your life choices, your self-assessment, and what you invite or allow into or keep out of your life?

5. Were there any family members you feared or were intimidated by? How has that been significant in your life since then, if at all?

6. What were the rules in your family about eating, cleaning up, dressing, and other parts of daily life? When you sat down to dinner, where did you sit, and what was expected of you?

7. Were there any family hero figures who had stories about them?

8. Were there any odd figures in your family who were ridiculed, such as a miser or a spendthrift, a noisy or overly talkative person, or a silent one?

9. What were the strengths and weaknesses in your family? How did they affect you?

10. Were there any events that made your family stronger or tore it apart?

11. What is the history of your family? What were its origins, and who were its major figures?

12. Did your family have a philosophy about life that was discussed and that you were expected to adopt? What were your family's "should" and "ought" messages? What favorite sayings illustrated your family or individual members of your family's philosophy of life?

13. Is there anything about your family that seemed or was unusual to you? Is there anything about your family that you wish had been different?

14. Is there something about your family that you hold dear and like to think about, remember?

15. What are some ways your family functioned that you carry over into your life now? If there is a particular lesson(s) you learned from your family, what is it?

16. What would be the book's title if one was written about your family?

WORK AND CAREER

Work is an integral part of life. What is your work story? Each of us spends our time doing things – by choice, chance, personal needs, the needs of others, what we are taught we should/ought/must do and be. Sometimes, we are fortunate to know, even from a young age, that our focus, work, and productive effort will go in a particular direction. As we do whatever it takes to move along that path, we find that choice is just right for us. Many others start on one path, find it works for a while or doesn't, and then move to another way, with or without angst by choice, chance, or necessity. What you do can bring purpose and meaning to your life or can be a way to keep you busy. As you reflect on how you have spent your time, what you value about where you have been, and what you have done, does this add up to work or a career that fits who you are and what you want for your life?

Ask yourself each question offered. Consider responding to a question(s) that makes you smile, that you are attracted to answering, and to one or two you don't like or want to turn away from. Facing what you don't like, or are uncomfortable with, is often a path to the most significant learning. These questions are guides to prime or stimulate your memories and thoughts about your life. The questions are not intended to be answered in a literal manner. Read through each of them and react to the one(s) that open windows for you. Each life is unique, and the priming questions impact each of us differently.

SENSITIZING QUESTIONS AND PROMPTS

1. What does life's work mean to you? What does career mean to you? Are they the same or something that changes over time?

2. When you were growing up, did you sense where you were headed and what your life's work would be? Did you have examples or models of people doing something that you thought was important? How did you know that? Did they tell you? Did it just seem that way?

3. Do you think one is called to do something? Are you called to be a teacher, a full-time parent, a doctor, an attorney, or whatever else? Are calling and purpose the same thing?

4. Do you get one chance to get it right? Is there one life's work for each person?

5. How do you know if you are doing your life's work now? If you are in the preparation phase of your life's work, are you appreciating and enjoying the process or just trying to get to where you are headed?

6. Can you change your mind and stop the path you are on if you see something more compelling? Is that giving up? Is that paying attention to what is suitable for you?

7. What is more important—child-rearing, working at a job or profession, creating something enduring, having experiences, gathering treasures, establishing relationships, developing a spiritual way of life, being kind, meeting your own needs, being authentic, and being strategic, or something else? What are your top choices if you are attracted to more than one of these possible life purposes? What is your order for them? Is that ordering consistent with what you have thought was your belief system?

8. Has gender impacted your life's work? Are women supposed to...? Are men supposed to...? Does that affect your work life if you are a gender-fluid person?

9. What is working when things are working for you in your life? What gives you the feeling of being on task, in the flow, living with purpose?

10. If you were starting your adult life now, how or what might be different for you than what you did? What is there to learn from that awareness? Does that impact how you think about your life's work?

11. What would you say if you were to say in just one sentence what your life's work is today?

12. If you were to say in just one sentence where your life is headed now regarding work, would that be different?

13. Are you ready to celebrate your life's work? How do you do that? Is there anyone you want to ask to join in that celebration?

14. Now what?

PURPOSE IN YOUR LIFE

In looking at your story — its details, your feelings, the good parts, and the other parts — see what you see, notice what you have been clear about and what is a surprise. Your story might center on being a parent, which has been your life's purpose, being an excellent parent. Or your story might be some particular aspect of that parent role that defines you. You taught your child to sing, dance, create, or something else. Your story might be that you are a professional something. Or your story might be the moments you did a particular thing that has the most meaning to you, perhaps to others, too, but it is how you see your purpose. Maybe your purpose is to bring beauty into the world or make the world better for your having been there. You might consider how that purpose has come to you and if that purpose continues to serve you. There is the doing, the noticing, the reflecting, the recommitting, and the savoring of your life's story and its purpose. What is your purpose?

Ask yourself each question offered. Consider responding to a question(s) that makes you smile, that you are attracted to answering, and to one or two you don't like or want to turn away from. Facing what you don't like, or are uncomfortable with, is often a path to the most significant learning. These questions are guides to prime or stimulate your memories and thoughts about your life. The questions are not intended to be answered in a literal manner. Read through each of them and react to the one(s) that open windows for you. Each life is unique, and the priming questions impact each of us differently.

SENSITIZING QUESTIONS AND PROMPTS

1. Purpose can mean gathering together what you have done that matters to you and others. What have you done in your life that matters to you and others? If you list those things, are they sufficient and good? Are they insufficient? Are they not so good? Have you been more selfish than you imagined? Have you been more giving than you realized? What about the balance between taking care of yourself vs. taking care of others?

2. Do you know someone, alive or dead, known or not, who has lived a life of purpose, a life you hold as a model? Who? What about that person(s) seems so valuable to you? What might you not do that might move your life more in the direction of that person who has such value to you?

3. Is there some profound guiding principle, idea, experience, or person that is part of your determination to do and move forward on the path you have chosen? Can you identify precisely what that principle is, who that person is, and what experience(s) coalesced to have you going forward the way you are?

4. Do you have any models of people you see or believe live a life of purpose? Is that the same or different from living a life of meaning?

5. Is having a purpose threat driven? That is, are you avoiding some feelings you do not want to have by having a purpose that others may value?

6. Do you want your life to have meaning? Are you fearful of life passing? Is finding or having a purpose a way to self-soothe?

7. If you do not have a purpose in your life, now, in the past, and in the future, is that okay with you? With the people around you who matter to you?

8. Is purpose a psychological idea that you would like to ignore? Is the concept uncomfortable for you in any way? How come?

9. What is the upside, in your mind, of focusing on your own life's purpose? If I know where I am headed, I have a better chance of getting there.

10. What is the downside in your mind of focusing on your purpose? For example, if I know where I am headed and don't get there, I'll feel worse than if I did not define what I am after. Is focusing on yourself being self-absorbed? Is that being too outcome driven? Is that taking you away from other things that matter to you more?

11. Has anyone influenced you about your purpose? Was that a positive influence? Was that a negative influence? Who did what? Is there any repair or recovery that needs to happen about who did or said what? Any things you want to say to that influencer by thanking them or whatever else?

12. If you were teaching/helping someone – your children, a close friend, a younger or older person in your life – to live a more purposeful life, how would you help? What would you say, suggest, direct, or offer?

13. Is a purpose-driven life a better way to live life? Is a spontaneous being in the flow of energy a better way to live? How would you compose and create that life if you could take elements from each?

14. Is a purposeful life a choice, chance, only something you see in retrospect, an intention, or something else?

15. Do you need to achieve a goal to live a good life? Do you need something you have defined as good to be accepted as having lived a good life?

16. Now what?

THE MEANING OF MONEY

Much is written about money; money means something different to each of us. Here are a few things we have been told about money all our lives. "There are people who have money and people who are rich." (Coco Chanel). "It is not the creation of wealth that is wrong, but the love of money for its own sake." (Margaret Thatcher). "Money is the root of all evil." (The Apostle Paul). "Money has never made man happy, nor will it; there is nothing in its nature to produce happiness. The more of it one has, the more one wants." (Benjamin Franklin) "It's a kind of spiritual snobbery that makes people think they can be happy without money." (Albert Camus) "I'd like to live as a poor man with lots of money." (Pablo Picasso) "I am opposed to millionaires, but it would be dangerous to offer me the position." (Mark Twain) "When I was young, I thought that money was the most important thing in life; now that I am old, I know that it is." (Oscar Wilde) What does money mean to you?

Ask yourself each question offered. Consider responding to a question(s) that makes you smile, that you are attracted to answering, and to one or two you don't like or want to turn away from. Facing what you don't like, or are uncomfortable with, is often a path to the most significant learning. These questions are guides to prime or stimulate your memories and thoughts about your life. The questions are not intended to be answered in a literal manner. Read through each of them and react to the one(s) that open windows for you. Each life is unique, and the priming questions impact each of us differently.

SENSITIZING QUESTIONS AND PROMPTS

1. Money – what does it mean to you? Do you need it? Do you want it? Do you have enough? Do you have too little? Is there ever too much? Does it give you status, power, self-esteem, security, safety, stress, envy, jealousy, or something else?

2. Do you have a significant, organizing belief or thought about money?

3. How much time do you spend thinking about, worrying about, or even counting your money? Is that okay with you? Is it a reasonable amount of time, too much, too little?

4. What is the connection, if any, between your self-esteem and how much money you earn, have accumulated, or have lost?

5. While growing up, what did you learn about money from the important people in your life — your parents, caregivers, and other family members? What were your mother's attitudes and teaching about money? What were your father's attitudes and education about money? Did they agree with each other? Did they fight about money? What was your takeaway from those observations and that learning? Was money scarce or plentiful in your family? Something else? How does that affect you today? Are you a saver? A spender? How come? Is that okay with you when you pause and take stock?

6. Were there clear messages about money? "Money is good." "Money is bad." "Money is power." "Spend." "Save." Were there confusing or indirect messages about money? What were they?

7. Does having money give you personal power? Power over others? Does not having money make you feel less than? How does that play out in your primary relationships, with friends, with acquaintances?

8. A common fear for women is becoming a "bag lady," a homeless woman who carries her possessions in shopping bags. Is that a fear for you? What do you do or think you should do to mitigate that fear?

9. Are you generous or stingy? Do you offer to pay the dinner bill with a friend? Does splitting a tab mean each person pays for just what they ate, or is 50-50 okay even if someone had more?

10. The proverbial question – if you win the lottery or a million dollars some other way, what then?

11. Money can be a key to self-knowledge. What does your relationship with money tell you about yourself?

12. If you had enough money, whatever that amount is, how would you change your life now?

13. What three lessons would you want to teach your children about money? What lessons about money and wealth do you wish you had learned when you were younger?

ACQUIRING MONEY

People define themselves by having money or not having money. More is better. Less is better. Some people compare themselves to others to define their success or equate their personal worth with their net worth. Some people find comfort in having enough, more than enough, and feel secure, happy, or even superior to others. Some think money corrupts, defines, has become too important, and divides and separates people. Having money is both a reality and an idea. Money is powerfully related to our memories and history, legacy, feelings, self-worth, opportunities, comfort, independence, control, options, and so much more.

Ask yourself each question offered. Consider responding to a question(s) that makes you smile, that you are attracted to answering, and to one or two you don't like or want to turn away from. Facing what you don't like, or are uncomfortable with, is often a path to the most significant learning. These questions are guides to prime or stimulate your memories and thoughts about your life. The questions are not intended to be answered in a literal manner. Read through each of them and react to the one(s) that open windows for you. Each life is unique, and the priming questions impact each of us differently.

SENSITIZING QUESTIONS AND PROMPTS

1. Can money buy you love? Have you given love to get money? As you think about that now, what thoughts and feelings do you have?

2. How did you acquire the money you have – earned it, married it, inherited it, won it, stole it, found it on the street, other? What are your thoughts about acquiring your assets?

3. Does money control you? Do you control it?

4. Can you talk about money openly? Do you know what your partner earns and how much that person has? Do they have that information about you? Is what are you doing with each other regarding sharing financial information working for you? Do you have hidden assets? How come they are hidden? What do you imagine would happen if the person found out you had more or less than they think or know?

5. Are you comfortable with money? Uncomfortable? Wary?

6. Where are you on the continuum of being interested in money to being obsessed with it: saving, getting the best deal, spending, living the fullest life, accumulating wealth, spending it all on your children and not yourself, giving it to causes and people, counting the pennies, investing, what else?

7. Are you addicted to money, that is, do you think about money constantly/too much as a way to avoid dealing with feelings about other issues in your life?

8. Do you have any models of people who handle money the way you think is right? Who are they, and what do you want to remember?

9. Is that okay with you if you make or have more money than someone with whom you are partnered? Is there anything about it that bothers you? Is there something you want/need to change to protect yourself? Does the difference impact how you think and feel about the person? Do you think you are loved more because you pay more or have more? If so, how is that?

10. Do you want more money than you have? How do you imagine your life would be different — better or worse — if you had more money? How might you get more money? Are you ready to do that? What steps would it take?

11. If you were suddenly much wealthier than you are today, what would change for you? What do you imagine would be most different if you suddenly lost your wealth?

12. Have you made any major money blunders, bad choices, or careless decisions? How difficult was that for you? What did you learn as a result? Has that learning changed things for you?

13. When you spend money on things, is it to buy what you need? Or is it to impress, to care for others, to soothe yourself, to indulge, all of these, or something else? Is that okay with you?

14. What has been your biggest or your most challenging purchase in life, your first and most challenging purchase? What can you observe today from the decisions to make those purchases?

15. If you buy something for yourself, can you use it right away, or do you need to do something to earn it and have it as a reward?

16. What gets you in trouble with money? Do you need something new to feel okay? Are you an accumulator, a hoarder, or an impulsive shopper?

17. What are the most robust and most powerful things you do regarding money? Do you save first, pay bills second, and then enjoy? Something else?

18. Do you lend money to people? Do you borrow money? How has that worked out?

19. Are you in control, out of control, overly controlled, or inadequately controlled about your spending?

20. What can money do? What can money not do?

21. Are you wealthy? Is that good? Is having money or valuing money somehow less than or not okay?

TALENTS: THE OLD, FORGOTTEN, WISHED FOR AND THE NEW AND YET TO BE

We define ourselves by what we are good at doing. The origins go back to childhood when we began defining ourselves. When our talents aligned with the goals of our family and the people around us, the development was most likely easy. But the experience may not have been so smooth if there was no match. Or, when our talents bump into gender constraints, there can be challenges. Not everyone is encouraged to pursue their dreams and talents as a child. What has been your experience finding your talents and defining your sense of competence?

Talent generally refers to one's natural ability or aptitude. Talent, though, can also relate to cultivated or learned skills and capacities. Once acquired, a talent can also be called a flair, a facility, a knack, expertise, a capacity, or a forte. There are talents our families wanted us to have, valued, and encouraged. Some talents were discounted or denied because they somehow did not fit what our caregivers valued. Sometimes, there is a collateral person — a teacher, a pastor/priest/rabbi, a scout leader, a neighbor — who encouraged us to do something different from what was desired in our family. That interest and resulting talent could have been viewed in a positive or not-so-positive way. Because of where, how, and from whom we explored our naturally occurring talents and those fostered in us, we usually come to have some array of talents/skills/capacities. Often there are also some denied, delayed, discounted talents that got discarded or ignored along the way. Reclaiming them can create an expanded or a very different life than if we did not turn toward them.

Ask yourself each question offered. Consider responding to a question(s) that makes you smile, that you are attracted to answering, and to one or two you don't like or want to turn away from. Facing what you don't like, or are uncomfortable with, is often a path to the most significant learning. These questions are guides to prime or stimulate your memories and thoughts about your life. The questions are not intended to be answered in a literal manner. Read through each of them and react to the one(s) that open windows for you. Each life is unique, and the priming questions impact each of us differently.

SENSITIZING QUESTIONS AND PROMPTS

1. What are your known talents? Make a list.

2. What are the talents you used to have? Make a list.

3. What talents do you wish you had? Make a list.

4. What defines or constitutes a talent?

5. What talents were recognized early in your life? Did your family recognize them? Friends? Others? Were they seen as positive, neutral, or negative?

6. Are there talents you had as a child and discarded along the way? How come? Who impacted that decision? Are those talents you would like to re-explore in your current life?

7. Were you encouraged to try new things? Or did your caregivers think you should play it safe and stick with the tried-and-true talents you possessed?

8. Were your desires realistic? For example, if you wanted to be the lead ballerina, did you have the physical abilities to match your passion?

9. Did your talents fit in with the plans your family had for you? Or did you have your own ideas about what was best for you? How was that received in your family? Did you have a champion who encouraged you? Or did you have a nay-sayer who discouraged you?

10. Did gender play a role in the development of your talents? Did you go outside the usual gender bounds?

11. What did you do while growing up to define what you were good at?

12. How did your childhood talents prepare you to fit into the world?

13. What are your talents over your lifetime? When and how did you find them?

14. Were your early talents expressed in your roles later in your life? How?

15. Did your most significant influence come from your parents? Friends? Your environment? Necessity?

16. Did your parents or caregivers have strong opinions about what talents you had or talents you "should" develop? Did they have opinions about any naturally occurring talents that should be ignored? Did you agree?

17. Is having a talent a good thing? A burden? What if you had talent but were not so interested in developing it?

18. Do you have a secret talent or the desire to develop a talent that you are reluctant, or embarrassed to say out loud? How come? What are you afraid might be said? By whom?

19. Is there someone you consider talented? Who? What are their talents? Does that person or those people have talents you wish you had? Do they handle their talent(s) well?

20. Can one develop a talent after age ____ (fill in the blank)?

21. If you have a talent, do you have to use it?

22. What is the measure of success with talent? Is it sufficient to just enjoy knowing you have that talent, or do you need to do something with it?

23. Who in your current life supports and encourages your talents? Who in your current life discourages or ignores your talents? What does that mean to you?

24. Do you need to find some cheerleader(s) or like-minded people with similar talents with whom to interact? Where would you start? What would you want from and with them?

25. Are talents always good? Are talents always or ever bad?

26. If there were no limits on time, money, physical ability, or anything else, what talents would you pursue? What do you imagine that would add to your life? What might that exploration replace?

27. How do your talents as a child reflect on the life you have now?

28. What things do you do well? Are those the same as your talents? Or how are they different?

29. How would your life be better if you explored, developed, and became immersed in a known, reclaimed, or new talent?

30. What would be the first step to expanding your talent?

31. Now, what?

CATEGORY II

THE CORE OF YOU

Your Inner Selves

Inner Critic

Giver and Taker

Feminine and Masculine – Gender Fluidity

Your essence, your inner self—feelings, thoughts, emotions, sensations—the parts of your interior life – impact who you are, what you do, what gets your attention, what direction you take, and your daily choices. Your profound stories of how you are in the world are continually impacted by your innermost self, whether in your awareness or unconscious. The themes in this category invite you to access those stories, those expressions of your individuality that describe and define you. These parts may seem invisible, but they show up in everything you do. Considering the stories about your core is a way to find, name, and know more and more and more about you, including your inner life.

YOUR INNER SELVES

Connection to your inner selves is what you know about yourself and what is less known, hidden, denied, or under-developed. What do you know about yourself? How do you define yourself? Who are you? What parts of you do you know, value and treasure? What parts of you are disliked and ignored? What experiences have you had that shaped who you are today? What values define you?

Connections to your deepest, inner self can be instinctive, that is, automatic, what you just do, what you may think of as what you have always done, or choice-full, that is, what happens after you have increased your awareness that there are parts of you that have been denied, underdeveloped, disliked, discouraged or not encouraged by your parents or caregivers.

Connecting to more of you, increasing your awareness of what defines you, and seeing or noticing if you are connecting to what you wish, want, imagine, and value can increase your awareness of your inner life. In a life with challenges — true for each of us —sometimes, reflection is put aside unless we are forced to look inside. Now, though, by choice, if you have decided to look inward — see what you see about you, feel what you like and don't, know, experience, consider, connect thoughtfully and carefully, and in an intuitive way — what to know about yourself — you can deepen your experience of you. Of course, the "trick" here is to get beyond your usual tale about yourself. For example, "You are a helper." The helper helps and may be trying to be seen, known, and appreciated. Or "you are a worker." So, you work, and perhaps you are also trying not to feel what you don't want to feel. Connections to your inner selves/parts, experiences, and values are the routes to greater awareness and more choices in your life.

Imagine this. You are the CEO of your life. Like any CEO, when you enter a new company, there are some departments for which you have a particular affinity. There are some departments you find less interesting or would prefer to ignore. As the CEO who wants the company to succeed, you will have to get familiar with every department to make decisions that will work for each department and the company. That is true for you, too. We need access to and appreciation for each part of us to create a good life. This process does not make life easier; surely, it makes life better.

For extensive reading about selves, look at the expansive, exquisite range of books, tapes, and more by Hal Stone, Ph.D. and Sidra Stone, Ph.D. https://www.voicedialogueinternational.com

Ask yourself each question offered. Consider responding to a question(s) that makes you smile, that you are attracted to answering, and to one or two you don't like or want to turn away from. Facing what you don't like, or are uncomfortable with, is often a path to the most significant learning. These questions are guides to prime or stimulate your memories and thoughts about your life. The questions are not intended to be answered in a literal manner. Read through each of them and react to the one(s) that open windows for you. Each life is unique, and the priming questions impact each of us differently.

SENSITIZING QUESTIONS AND PROMPTS

1. What do you just know about yourself? What is the answer to the question, "Who are you?" How does that match up with whom you want to be? For example, if "who you are" is someone's mother or business partner, what do you think about that role/function? Is there an upside and a downside, too? What connections are missing when you see your answers to that question?

2. Are you connected to your inner self? What does that mean to you?

3. Do you allow yourself to know what works and does not work for you? Are you heavily invested in a particular version of yourself, a well-known story/tale/history/narrative others created for you? What would you say if you were to create the story of what you want your life to be now without worrying about the impact on others?

4. What are you longing for in your life? When we wish for something — for example, to be seen, known, and appreciated, or to be liked, loved and cared for, or to be listened to and respected, or something else, that wishing or longing is often a way for us to know that we must do something other/different than we are doing to feel connected to ourselves in the way we want to be. What are you longing for?

5. 5. What do you judge others as very positive or negative? Those judgments are clear routes to finding out more about you. The bigger the judgment, the bigger the learning. Judgments tell us there is something in us that needs to be developed. If you judge someone who takes care of themselves as "selfish," that could mean that you are not taking good enough care of yourself. What do you judge in others, and what do you have to learn about yourself from those judgments?

6. What shows up in your dreams—nighttime dreams and daydreams? Our dreams often reveal exactly what we do not want to let ourselves see or know about ourselves. Do you "hear" and "see" your dreams? If so, what might they be offering to you? If you do not recall dreams, are you willing to invite them in by telling yourself at night, "I want to remember my dream." Dreams are a significant resource in knowing more about yourself. Ignoring your dreams may have significant negative consequences.

7. Experiences define us, too. They offer a connection to what you value, enjoy, appreciate, avoid, fear, or somewhere in between. What experiences are you drawn to, and what do you ignore, reject, or avoid? If you pause and consider your choices, are they good ones for you? If not, what would be better? If so, time to celebrate!

8. If you can get beyond what you like and do not like about yourself and ask the question, "what would make me more of what I care to be," what comes to mind? What are the ways you might be more of whatever that is? What gets in your way? What steps might you take to move forward in a way that helps you feel there is the possibility and hope to be more?

9. How do you experience inner peace and connection to what some people call their soul? How do you get in your way and miss that connection to your inner life?

10. Are there experiences you have had that are so pivotal in your life that they have shaped your fundamental way of being? What are those experiences? Whether you think of them as positive or not, what has been the learning from them that has impacted your life over time?

11. What would you say to yourself ten years from now about how you want to be and what you want in your life? What moves you in that direction? What gets in the way or distracts you from moving toward that future desired self?

12. What supports your growth? What gets in the way of your expanded view of yourself?

13. If you are truly connected to the person you are — the parts you love and cherish, the parts that are hidden/denied/underdeveloped, the parts you do not like, all the parts of you, then how could your life be different than it is today? How would it be the same?

14. What do you celebrate in your connection to yourself now — not the public self, but your inner self?

15. Who supports your connection to being all of you? Who doesn't? What does that mean to you?

16. Can you be loved with access to parts of you that even you do not like? Can you create an accepting way to think of yourself with all you value and with all you wish was not true?

17. What does today's experience bring you that was not in your awareness before now?

18. What thought, feeling, idea of yourself, or expression of yourself do you want to take away from this time with yourself and time with the people you have cared about for many years?

INNER CRITIC

What is there to learn from your inner critic? How has it protected you? What is its deep value? Most of us have an inner critic, that part of ourselves that can run in our heads 24/7 telling us things about ourselves and making judgments about us that are often hard to hear. The inner critic sometimes calls us an imposter, "If people only knew who I am," and we experience this as the "imposter syndrome," just waiting to be found out that we are not what we seem to be. The inner critic can stop you from trying things, saying things, doing things that you want to do but are afraid of doing poorly, and feeling bad or foolish. Being a beginner at something, especially as an adult, is a challenge, and if you can be a beginner, life has endless options. The inner critic is valuable and helpful. That critic is a protector, a part of ourselves that wants to be sure we are seeing things about us that we may not want to see, both good and perhaps not so good. The problem is often that the inner critic delivers the message harshly or painfully. That could be because we do not want to hear what that critic is trying to say, so the voice inside of us gets bigger and louder. If you write down what the inner critic is telling you and sort out what is essential to consider and what is just mean, you may have a road map to self-discovery, healing, and more options in your life.

Ask yourself each question offered. Consider responding to a question(s) that makes you smile, that you are attracted to answering, and to one or two you don't like or want to turn away from. Facing what you don't like, or are uncomfortable with, is often a path to the most significant learning. These questions are guides to prime or stimulate your memories and thoughts about your life. The questions are not intended to be answered in a literal manner. Read through each of them and react to the one(s) that open windows for you. Each life is unique, and the priming questions impact each of us differently.

SENSITIZING QUESTIONS AND PROMPTS

1. Do you have an inner critic? How do you know? Can you describe it? What does it say to you? What is your relationship with it?

2. Is that a part of you that you are well aware lives inside of you? What is your experience with it? Has it helped? Has it stopped you? What are some examples? Is it time to reconsider?

3. Growing up, you probably heard good things about yourself, critical things about you, and everything in between. Does your inner critic mimic the voices and messages of those who were or are in your life? What are those familiar messages, and from whom?

4. Are some of the messages from your inner critic ideas that help you, protect you, and offer you thoughts that would be useful for you to consider?

5. Is the message delivery from that inner critic gentle or harsh, sometimes one and sometimes the other?

6. What is an example of a message your inner critic has brought you that was something you needed to hear even if you didn't particularly want to hear it? What is an example of a message from your inner critic that was just mean, hurtful, and not useful for you? How can you separate them?

7. Knowing what we don't know about ourselves is a challenge. What ways have you found to access those parts of you that you do not access right now?

8. If you select one or more of the inner critic messages and write about it with an open mind, what do you imagine could come from that deep dive, that frank look at yourself? Just one message. Just one to start.

9. How might your life be better if you sifted and sorted the mean inner critic messages from the helpful messages?

10. Can you imagine letting yourself listen to your inner critic and consider what it is saying to you, being a positive life-altering choice? Just let yourself wonder.

GIVER AND TAKER/ HELPER AND RECEIVER. GOOD, BAD, MAKING CHOICES

Some people, and many women, are socialized to help, support, nurture, encourage, accommodate, do for, do more, offer, listen, please, and give. As with any aspect of oneself, there are enhancing, positive aspects of being the helper, and there are limiting, negative parts. Take stock and look clearly at where you are on the continuum of helping others vs. helping yourself first or at all; notice where you are on the continuum of offering help, asking for help, receiving help, taking care of yourself. Many people are so accustomed to showing up for others that it feels awkward, selfish, bad to pause, stop or even consider their choices before suggesting, volunteering, saying, doing. The idea that not doing may be a better choice, the good choice, is foreign, uncomfortable, and to be avoided.

For some people, the opposite is true. Making sure you are taken care of first, or maybe only taking care of you is right and good. Taking is desirable. Giving not so much. Frequently givers/helpers are magnets for takers. The homeostasis of life requires that a taker has a helper to help. Life needs to be in balance, not necessarily equal or even, but with the choice, you can be both a helper and a receiver. Only when a helper can help or take care of themself does the taker move on because now, the taker would be required to give. There are relationships where each person is learning to access and express the opposite parts of themselves, often because of distress with the people in their lives. The other person becomes the teacher, whether you wish that to be true or not. Take note of where your relationships are on this continuum. This question can stir deep feelings if you face it directly and honestly. Bravely let yourself go to where your inner wisdom takes you.

Ask yourself each question offered. Consider responding to a question(s) that makes you smile, that you are attracted to answering, and to one or two you don't like or want to turn away from. Facing what you don't like, or are uncomfortable with, is often a path to the most significant learning. These questions are guides to prime or stimulate your memories and thoughts about your life. The questions are not intended to be answered in a literal manner. Read through each of them and react to the one(s) that open windows for you. Each life is unique, and the priming questions impact each of us differently.

SENSITIZING QUESTIONS AND PROMPTS

1. Is a giver and a helper the same? Are a taker and a receiver the same? What does that mean if you think of being a "giver" or a "taker"? What does a giver do or not do? What does a taker do or not do?

2. Do you have an internal response to the question of whether you are a giver or a taker? What is that response? Is that a known part of you, a surprise?

3. In your logical, thinking mind, where would you like to be on the continuum of the giver to taker? How come? Is that different from being a helper to a receiver?

4. Of the people in your life, if you made a frank list of who is more on the giver side and who is more on the taker side, without trying to be "nice" or "correct" and without letting anyone off the hook, who would be on which side? How is that when you look at the list you made?

5. What are three examples in your current life when you give? When you take? When you receive? What is the ratio of giving to taking?

6. How well do you ask specifically and directly for what you want and need? Do you comfortably receive good words, thoughts, and deeds from others? What is an example of a time when you were fully available to accept what was offered? How was that for you? Good? Bad? Odd? Confusing? Destabilizing? Other?

7. Do you ignore reality? If someone says they are doing something for you and it feels good, do you let those feelings in? If someone says they are doing something for you and it feels bad because of whatever, do you allow those feelings in, or do you make excuses and deny the reality?

8. Does helping feel good? Does helping feel bad? What is distinct in the situations where you feel polar opposite feelings? Are there particular circumstances or people for whom helping is positive? Are there specific people or circumstances for whom helping is negative, but you keep doing it? How come? What would happen if you stopped? What happens if you keep helping/giving?

9. What is sufficient helping? Do you ask yourself that question? What would be different if you let yourself consider that question?

10. What does being selfish mean? Who is selfish in your life? Are you selfish? What did you learn growing up about being selfish? Did you learn that sharing is a good thing? Did you learn that helping makes you a good person? What else did you learn? Is taking care of yourself good or bad, something not even mentioned growing up? Was your Mother a giver, a helper, a taker, a receiver? Was your Father a giver, a helper, a taker, a receiver? What did that teach you? Was there another caregiver/family friend/neighbor who influenced this area?

11. If being a giver or a helper is good, and there are people close to you who are takers or receivers, how come that is okay for them but not for you?

12. Are takers liars/manipulators who say they are givers/helpers? Are givers/helpers martyrs?

13. If you were to set an intention for yourself to move toward the end of the continuum that is less known now, what intention would you set? What kind of pushback, turn-back, would you anticipate from people around you who are used to your being a certain way? How would you take care of yourself if you got some pushback, you did not like?

14. Do you get tired of helping or giving? When? With whom? Do you get tired of taking or receiving? When? With whom?

15. Is there any person you know who seems to have the ratio of helping, taking, and self-care that seems right to you? What can you learn from that person?

16. When you think of setting limits, is that tolerable, positive, or negative? When?

17. Considering this question of giver and helper vs. taker and receiver, what are your current thoughts? How have they changed as a result of this consideration?

18. What are your next steps? Now what?

FEMININE AND MASCULINE. MASCULINE AND FEMININE. GENDER FLUIDITY

By genetic type, perhaps we are more of a female or more of a male. By preferences and behaviors, we are more of a male or more of a female. When you take stock of who you are and how you are in your world, are you more female than male or male than female? While we all have predispositions to being somewhere on the continuum from macho to girly girly, most of what we think, feel, and do is instinctive. For this writing, consider where you are on the spectrum and if/how you live your life by choice, chance, or default. Adding in, reducing, or eliminating choices can pull/push you into more of the life you want. Gender fluidity, an openly discussed and clear choice for people to make, allows us to find, say, and be who we want and need to be.

Ask yourself each question offered. Consider responding to a question(s) that makes you smile, that you are attracted to answering, and to one or two you don't like or want to turn away from. Facing what you don't like, or are uncomfortable with, is often a path to the most significant learning. These questions are guides to prime or stimulate your memories and thoughts about your life. The questions are not intended to be answered in a literal manner. Read through each of them and react to the one(s) that open windows for you. Each life is unique, and the priming questions impact each of us differently.

SENSITIZING QUESTIONS AND PROMPTS

1. How do you define masculinity or femininity? Who taught you that definition? What is gender fluidity?

2. As you begin to write, are you closer to one end of the spectrum than the other? How can you tell? Is that okay with you? Is that okay for the people who matter to you in your life? If so, how is that? If not, then what?

3. If five people who know you well were to place you on that same continuum, would they see you the way you see yourself? Maybe it would be helpful to ask. Or not?

4. Choose one or two significant people—how would each of those people describe you in terms of femininity/masculinity?

5. With those assessments in mind, what works for you and what doesn't?

6. If you were going to add in one or more characteristics of the opposite side, where would you start? What would that look like to you?

7. Do you have fears, doubts, and concerns about adding in some feminine or masculine characteristics? For whom would that change be an issue? For whom would that change be a welcome adjustment?

8. If you think of your life twenty years from now, what is essential for you to be experiencing currently regarding your masculine and feminine parts?

9. When you think of someone feminine, what words would you use to describe that person?

10. When you think of someone masculine, what words would you use to describe that person?

11. If you wanted to add something (s) new to how you live your life that would make you feel more masculine or feminine, what would you add, beginning when?

12. Do you believe the world around you responds differently to you because you are physically female or male? What would you change about how you present yourself to enhance or mitigate that response?

13. If you had a genetically male or a genetically female child, what would you want to say to them about that fact?

14. Is there something you wish you had known about being feminine or masculine ten or more years ago that would have informed how you lived the last years? What does that say to you about the next ten or more years?

15. If you were beginning a correspondence with someone without having met them and you introduced yourself as feminine or masculine, what would you be hoping to tell them about yourself?

16. If you could simply choose to be more masculine or feminine, what would be different about you today and from now on?

CATEGORY III

CHOICE POINTS

Where Have You Been in Your Life?

Pivotal Moments

How Will You Remember?

Gifts: Giving, Receiving, Tangible, Intangible

We come to a fork in the road and choose an option. These are deciding moments that take us one way or the other. Sometimes that choice resonates, is clear, sure, and accessible. More times, though, there are options to consider, weigh—which we do or don't do—and then see what happens. Often, we have to surrender to the outcome and how those choices turn out. Turning toward, looking at those choice points, whether they turned out the way we imagined, hoped for, thought we wanted and needed, or didn't, define us. These themes are a chance to consider the stories that are crucial and significant to the person you are. Whether they worked the way you thought they would, or something close to that, or something even dramatically different happened, your life may become more known, understood, and appreciated as you collect these stories.

You may notice that some themes have more questions than others. These themes and questions were organic in how they were created. There is no intention or implication that one theme is more worthy than another for you to address.

WHERE HAVE YOU BEEN IN YOUR LIFE?

Days, weeks, and months of one's life can blend with barely an awareness that time is passing. We may organize our recollections around milestones, highlights, big birthday numbers, world events, celebratory occasions, or something else. Most of life, though, is what we experience, think about, do, and feel each day. Noticing where you have been is a way to pause, collect, consider, collate, and organize your life in whatever way helps you see what is important to you. You might be someone who has a bucket list of things done and to do that constitute a good life. You might be someone who does not have a bucket list and doesn't even like that idea because it takes something away from how you want to live your life.

Celebrating others is frequently important. Celebrating one's self is less regularly a goal. Celebrating big things gets many people's attention — beginnings and endings (e.g., a new child, a new dog, a new house, a new committed relationship, a new something, or a graduation, a move, or completion of a major project). Some holidays mean something important to some people.

Take time to notice where you have been, what you attend to, and if those choices are what is good and right for you. If they are, wonder if there is a way to enhance further and enjoy what, who, and how those things are part of your life. If the choices are off just a bit, then what? If you see, with reflection, that you are just doing what you have always done, what your family did, just what you know people do, what others expect/need/want, consider what might be a more choice-full, personally enriching way to live your life.

Ask yourself each question offered. Consider responding to a question(s) that makes you smile, that you are attracted to answering, and to one or two you don't like or want to turn away from. Facing what you don't like, or are uncomfortable with, is often a path to the most significant learning. These questions are guides to prime or stimulate your memories and thoughts about your life. The questions are not intended to be answered in a literal manner. Read through each of them and react to the one(s) that open windows for you. Each life is unique, and the priming questions impact each of us differently.

SENSITIZING QUESTIONS AND PROMPTS

1. What would be its title if you were to write a book about your life? What is an alternative? Or two alternatives? What do you think? Is that the life you want to be living? What would you include and exclude if you were to make a small collage that captured your life?

2. If you were to title a book about the life you want to live or want to have lived, what would be its title? What elements might you include in a small collage describing the theme or themes you want in this intended life?

3. How do you organize your life — event-driven? Decade or time-driven? Internally driven? Externally driven? Who was around when? What you accomplished? How you suffered? How you soared? Something else?

4. What would be the key elements to include if you make a timeline for your life? If there are images that capture those elements, what would they be? Are there things that have gone on in your life to ignore? Do you have a central organizing principle of what is in and what is out? Do you need one? Do you want one?

5. As you reflect on where you have been, what feelings/thoughts/sensations/memories/ideas come to mind? How is that for you? Satisfying? Disturbing? Surprising? Comforting? Peaceful? Stimulating? All of those? What else? Perhaps, you are content and just glad to be noticing. Maybe you are discontented and want to make sure of something. What is that?

6. Is what you experience, as you reflect, okay with you? Where does it lead you, if anywhere? Is noticing sufficient?

7. What says to you that you are living the life you choose? What says to you that you are not? Is whatever is true for you okay with you? If not, then what?

8. What makes a good life? Do you have all, some, enough, not enough of whatever makes a good life? Now what?

9. What describes the good life for you if you let yourself be quiet and still, even for a moment or two? What key images, descriptors, and ideas say to you, "This is right for me"?

10. Then, there are celebrations. Some people might call them rituals, the ordinary things they do at certain times, what the world does on December 25th or Yom Kippur. What do you call the times of your life that are extra important to you? How come they are?

11. What does it give you to have rituals, celebrations, and regular times that are not daily?

12. Does the idea of celebrating every day make intellectual sense, emotional sense, or no sense to you? Is it a concept? Does it have resonance with you?

13. If you were celebrating every day, would that become routine? Is that okay? How could you do that if you wanted to celebrate each day? Would that be one more thing to do or something valuable and positive for you?

14. There is the idea that each person needs some way(s) they can count on to generate good feelings that do not include anyone else. Do you agree with that idea? Do you have ways that you celebrate you, your everyday?

15. Do you have ways you celebrate you on any schedule? If you make a collage, what would you include? Exclude? While you might think this is a good idea, is there any chance this will happen? How can you remember?

16. Do you think it is a wrong/selfish/a poor place to put energy into creating "celebrations" for yourself? Would you tell anyone? Who? Would they support you? If not, then what?

17. What have you celebrated in the past? Was it the best way for you to do that celebrating? If not, how come? What is there to learn from that experience?

18. When is it time to start celebrating whatever you are going to celebrate?

19. What is one sentence that best describes what a positive and rich celebration means to you? Have you had them? Can you plan one now? Will you create it?

20. Now, what? What is your next step as you review, reflect, celebrate, and create a collage, a story, or a moment to consider?

PIVOTAL MOMENTS AND THEIR MEANING

As you tune into your life today, what expectations, thoughts, beliefs, and ideas about yourself do you bring? Take a moment to consider at least one description or a sense of yourself that you are carrying right now. For example, you could be saying to yourself, "I am young/old and therefore…." Or "I am smart/not as smart as others, likable/not so likable, better than/not as good as someone else here today, and therefore…(what)?"

Those thoughts/ideas/beliefs about yourself are likely the result of your experiences. Do they still fit or not? Are they instinctive, automatic ideas about yourself that you carry without considering if they work for you now? If they fit, now, okay. If not, what image, or view of yourself, would you like to cultivate? A way to create personal images is with collaged SoulCollage* cards, or if you prefer, write about the desired place you want to move toward.

*Your SoulCollage® Deck is the Story of You. Create a unique deck of colorful, collaged SoulCollage® cards with deep personal meaning. See www.SoulCollage.com

As we move through our lives, there are events/experiences — big and small — that impact our lives. Sometimes we know, at the time, that what is or has happened will have a profound or meaningful impact on us and our sense of who we are. Sometimes, we only realize retrospectively that an event or experience has been pivotal. There are changes in any life — of circumstance and fortune — that we like and those that we don't. As a result of what you have experienced, consider your central organizing principle, theme, primary belief about who you are, or a filter that defines who you are. How do you describe or think of yourself, the thread of who you are that runs through your life? Some people define themselves by their significant roles — parent/a non-parent, single/married/divorced, worker/career person, a talent, an image, a future something or something else. As you think about what has happened in your life, how have these pivotal events impacted, shaped, and determined your idea of who you are?

Ask yourself each question offered. Consider responding to a question(s) that makes you smile, that you are attracted to answering, and to one or two you don't like or want to turn away from. Facing what you don't like, or are uncomfortable with, is often a path to the most significant learning. These questions are guides to prime or stimulate your memories and thoughts about your life. The questions are not intended to be answered in a literal manner. Read through each of them and react to the one(s) that open windows for you. Each life is unique, and the priming questions impact each of us differently.

SENSITIZING QUESTIONS AND PROMPTS

1. What are big, defining life events/experiences in your life? What events/experiences that, at the time, you thought were small but had a significant impact on you and your life?

2. Have the pivotal events/experiences in your life developed into a pattern or theme for your life? As a result of what has happened in your life, do you have a belief, a filter, or a definition of who you are?

3. Is there a belief, filter, or self-definition that tells you who you are? What is it? Has it changed over time? Is it something you like and feel good about or not? Is it something you accept? Do others know this about you?

4. Is there a theme, defining idea about you that you wish was true for you, but it isn't, at least not now?

5. Is what others know about you, see in you, what you know and see about yourself? Or do others see you very differently from how you see yourself? How come? Is that okay? Or not?

6. Sometimes, something has happened that we don't want to be true, that we want to ignore, delete from our mind, not say, not tell, almost not know. Whether you write about that or not, read about that or not, how has the "secret" informed or defined you? For example, does the "secret" make you feel separate, alone, not seen, or different from others? Do you feel superior or inferior because this happened? What do you imagine would happen if people knew this about you? How does it define you?

7. Positive, impressive moments can be a joy or a burden. Do you talk about your fabulous achievements, accolades, and successes, or do you keep those secret? How come? Who would you want to tell other than the people who already know?

8. How do the very positive things you have experienced or the very negative or difficult things you have had in your life define you? Are positives more defining or the challenges? How come?

9. We all have core needs that motivate or direct us. That might be — security needs, belonging or connecting needs, power needs, needs to be seen/heard, or protecting yourself and others. How do your basic needs show up in your life's pivotal events/experiences?

10. What are the primary motivators, desires, and wishes you recognize that have been a part of your life over time? Are they the same now? Different? What caused the change?

11. Is there some similarity in these significant events? For example, are most events initiated by you or have you reacted, or responded to circumstances? Is whatever you did or didn't do okay with you? That is if you were typically the initiator, do you wish you would have been more willing to follow others at times? Or, if you primarily respond to what comes your way, do you imagine taking the lead for yourself would have been a better choice?

12. Are these pivotal times for you associated with relationships? Losses? Accomplishments? Do these events cluster around a specific time period, or are they spread throughout your life?

13. Were there wishes/dreams/hopes catalysts for these life events? What were those wishes/dreams/hopes?

14. Did these pivotal life events come out of desire, duty, being the "good" person, the "bad" person, or some other definition of you? What is the proportion of each? Are you surprised? Have you been aware, all along, that you are the way you are?

15. If you define yourself as a . . . (fill in the blank), is that a good thing or not? How come?

16. As you take stock and look at these pivotal life events, in a line or two, what do you see is the description of you now? Do you want that definition to continue, expand, contract, change slightly, change completely, go away, or something else?

17. Now what?

HOW WILL YOU REMEMBER? YOUR BELIEF, FILTER, DEFINITION OF WHO YOU ARE

Many of us have defining moments, and we say to ourselves that this changes everything. We are sure we'll remember what made this time so significant. We may even promise ourselves or others that, as a result, we'll do or not do, say, or not say something different than we did before. That might just happen, that we remember. And it might not. In thinking about what you have experienced and learned, how will you remember what you want to remember? For example, one person said, "My divorce is so terrible; I promise that if I find another person to be in a relationship with, I'll do whatever it takes to keep that relationship. I never want to get divorced again." In the next relationship, issues came up, and she worked hard, very hard, to resolve them. When something that felt terrible happened, she remembered what she had told herself and worked it through so she could have what she wanted.

Ask yourself each question offered. Consider responding to a question(s) that makes you smile, that you are attracted to answering, and to one or two you don't like or want to turn away from. Facing what you don't like, or are uncomfortable with, is often a path to the most significant learning. These questions are guides to prime or stimulate your memories and thoughts about your life. The questions are not intended to be answered in a literal manner. Read through each of them and react to the one(s) that open windows for you. Each life is unique, and the priming questions impact each of us differently.

SENSITIZING QUESTIONS AND PROMPTS

1. How do you remember what you want to remember? Do you have a way?

2. Do you find that you repeat the same things you wish you hadn't repeatedly? How come? What is there to learn?

3. Do you see or know people who seem able to learn from what has happened in their lives, be it something wonderful or terrible? How did they do it? What can you learn from them? Want to ask that person?

4. What did you observe from your family of origin? Did they keep doing destructive things? Did they learn and change and grow?

5. There is the idea that people may have to sink to the bottom of their pain to be able to make and sustain changes that will be better for them. Is that what you think? Has that been true for you or the people around you?

6. Right now, what do you remember, recall, and remind yourself would be useful and helpful for you to remember about what is important to you? For example. Kindness in a relationship is at the top of the list of what I need. Or leave the place where I just was better than when I arrived.

7. If you reflect on repeating self-limiting behaviors, what are they? Can you name them? List them? Do you need help with challenging them so you can make new choices?

8. What help can you imagine might assist you in remembering what you know, believe, hope, or feel would be good to have accessible and even become more instinctive?

GIFTS: GIVING, RECEIVING, TANGIBLE, INTANGIBLE

Some people love gifts, giving and receiving them often and well. Some people don't think giving or receiving gifts is all that terrific because, for them, the whole idea of gifts is confusing, challenging, guilt-producing, uninspiring, or just plain too much to handle! Like most things people do, there is a range of how we experience and perceive this complicated part of life. Some among us are more generous. Others are more equalizers and keep track of who gave what. For some, that informs what we should give. Some people give too much. Others are withholding. Some people have a feeling of abundance in their lives and want to share that feeling. Other people have a sense of scarcity and live within that constraint. One person wants to receive gifts but is not so good at giving. Finding where you are on this continuum is clarifying. Some people expect gifts, need gifts, want gifts, big gifts, any kind of gift, the right gift. Others are content to ask for their basic needs to be met in receiving a gift — "I'll be happy if you take out the trash each week. That will let me know you care about me." Others want the grand gift, the grand gesture.

Genuinely receiving a gift can be wonderful or otherwise. Many relish the presents they receive, whether they are objects, behaviors, or words. Some people are uncomfortable or are so deeply moved by the gift-receiving experience, even if it is a small gesture, that they are filled with tears. Of course, anytime you have an emotional response to something in your life, this is a cue, a signal, that something is happening within you that may be worth turning toward, fully engaging with, and from which you can learn.

Ask yourself each question offered. Consider responding to a question(s) that makes you smile, that you are attracted to answering, and to one or two you don't like or want to turn away from. Facing what you don't like, or are uncomfortable with, is often a path to the most significant learning. These questions are guides to prime or stimulate your memories and thoughts about your life. The questions are not intended to be answered in a literal manner. Read through each of them and react to the one(s) that open windows for you. Each life is unique, and the priming questions impact each of us differently.

SENSITIZING QUESTIONS AND PROMPTS

1. Are you better at giving or receiving a gift? How do you know? What pivotal experience(s) relates to giving or getting a gift?

2. What does a gift you are giving say about you? What should it say? Does it matter?

3. Should the gift you give be more about you, the giver, or the recipient?

4. How much should you spend on a gift? More than you can afford to make a big statement? What you can afford? Should a gift be a token? Where are you on this spectrum?

5. If the recipient never gives you a gift, is it okay to keep giving? Why? When? What is the message? What does it say about you? If the recipient never thanks you, do you keep on giving? Does it depend on who it is?

6. Do you give gifts for a reason? Are there good reasons for giving a gift? Are there bad reasons for giving a gift? What is or are your reasons— for expressing caring or love? To be loved? To be valued? To be

accepted? To get a gift in return? To show your status? To celebrate a person or occasion? Because you are expected to give a gift? Because of what?

7.   Is re-gifting an option? If so, when? What are the acceptable parameters? Do you have an experience of re-gifting or receiving a re-gift? What happens if you find out or the receiver of your gift finds out? Have you had an awkward moment where the "secret" re-gifting was discovered? e.g., you left the card in the package from the person who initially gave you the gift?

8.   What about the gift lists some people and some families think are the answer to giving gifts that are truly wanted? Is that a good idea? Why? Is that a poor idea? Why? Must you give the gifts that are on the list the potential recipient made? What if you don't like any of the items noted?

9.   There are gift registries for many events/occasions — weddings, showers, anniversaries, graduations, etc. Are those mandatory? Is this an ethics question, that is, what is the right thing to do?

10. When you receive a gift, what are your responsibilities, if any? Do you meet those obligations? Do you send thank you notes, or is a verbal acknowledgment adequate? What do you expect of the recipient if you are the gift giver? What is an adequate expression of appreciation?

11. What if you do not like the gift you received? Then what? Has that happened? How did you handle it? Did you like the giver less because they missed the mark with you? Think twice about this question!

12. Does the exchange of gifts influence your relationship with the giver or the receiver? If so, how? As you observe your response, what do you learn about yourself?

13. When is giving a gift not giving a gift, if ever?

14. What is the favorite gift you have ever given? What is the best gift you have ever received? Say more.

15. Is giving gifts to yourself giving a gift?

16. Who is the best gift giver in your life? How come? Who is the poorest gift giver? What might you do about that, if anything?

17. In many relationships —families, friendships, parent-child, partners—gift giving is fraught with challenges. What have you experienced about gift giving and receiving in any of these relationships? What is there to observe? How do you mitigate the difference if you are great at gift giving and your partner is lousy or not so good?

18. What is your perfect gift to give? Has it happened?

19. What is your perfect gift to receive? Has it happened?

20. Does price matter when you give a gift? Should it? What does it say if it does?

21. Can gift giving ever be aggressive or hostile? How so? Have you been the aggressor or the recipient of such an experience? What is there to learn as you think about that now? Is advice-giving a gift?

22. Do you keep gifts you don't want? Can you toss an expensive gift in the trash? Of course? Of course, not? Give it away?

23. You see the perfect gift for someone, and there is no occasion. Now what?

24. Does accepting a gift make you indebted to the gift giver?

25. Do you give too many gifts? Not enough?

26. What is a grand gesture? Have you been the recipient of one? How was/is that for you? Have you been the giver? How was/is that for you?

27. What are the gifts you wish you had given? Wish to give?

28. There are small gifts and large gifts. What is your style?

29. What are ways you might want to expand your generous self? What are ways you might want to limit your generous self?

30. Some people give gifts to strangers. Is that you? Do you want it to be you?

31. Some people give gifts to the people they encounter in everyday life—the doctor, the lawyer, the mail person, the teacher, the neighbor. Is that you? Do you want it to be you?

32. Some people do not give gifts, or many, for all sorts of reasons. Make your best case for giving fewer gifts.

33. If you were going to write a gift-giving plan for yourself going forward, what would it say?

34. Is giving gifts a fun and positive experience for you? Is giving gifts stressful, complicated, challenging, annoying or something else?

35. There is a song Barbara Cook sings that says, giving to you takes nothing away from me. Do you agree? What is there to learn from that sentiment? (The actual lyrics are not available.)

36. Do you like people who give you gifts better than people who don't? Do people like you better if you give them gifts?

37. What are the limits? What are your boundaries about gifts? For example. Do not give gifts unless you want to give a gift. Do not receive a gift unless you want to receive it. Do not take gifts from people who are otherwise not kind to you. Only give or receive gifts from people with whom you want a close relationship. What are your limits?

38. What do you teach your children about giving gifts to you and others?

39. Do you have a central value for gift giving?

40. Is there someone you want to give a gift to now? Will you?

CATEGORY IV

RELATIONSHIPS

Relationships: The Good, the Troubles, What Needs Attention

Children and Pets

Connections

Friendships: The Sweetness And The Pain

Personal Boundaries: Where, When, and How To Draw The Line

Heroes/Heroines and Villains

Romance: Who Were/Are They, Those Romantic People In Your Life

Relationships are basic to life; they are great or good, so-so, painful, or awful, and every step along the continuum. Every single connection, for the moment or the lifetime, can change us in simple to profound ways. What we learn from our critters—noticing how they are—to what we experience with our families, mentors, friends, and even passing connections can make all the difference in how we experience and live life. Your stories that come from these themes are major, substantive, significant, and often describe who you are most fundamentally. Read the themes and see if you have an affinity for one theme or a rejection of another theme. Just notice what moves you forward in knowing more about who you are. There are surely stories to tell.

RELATIONSHIPS: THE GOOD, THE TROUBLES, WHAT NEEDS ATTENTION

Most of us want personal relationships. Few among us prefer to be alone all the time. Being close to other people is a deep need, so profound that most of us cannot live without being involved with others. And yet, close relationships are complicated. Think about your hopes and dreams for your connection with others. Notice where you have fulfilled those wishes and where there are ongoing or new desires, and longings. Rarely is there someone who says that they are totally content, all the time, with the quality, depth, and range of the connections they have. What do you celebrate? Whom do you celebrate? Do they know? Do they know what doesn't work for you? What troubles you and might need or does need attention? What is there to do, think, or feel to have close/closer relationships?

Ask yourself each question offered. Consider responding to a question(s) that makes you smile, that you are attracted to answering, and to one or two you don't like or want to turn away from. Facing what you don't like, or are uncomfortable with, is often a path to the most significant learning. These questions are guides to prime or stimulate your memories and thoughts about your life. The questions are not intended to be answered in a literal manner. Read through each of them and react to the one(s) that open windows for you. Each life is unique, and the priming questions impact each of us differently.

SENSITIZING QUESTIONS AND PROMPTS

1. What is a good relationship? Do you have a good relationship with anyone, someone? How do you know? What do the people around you say to you about your relationship with them? What do you tell yourself about the relationships you have — be they family, friends, romantic, casual, intense, hoped for, whatever kind?

2. Do you define yourself by the relationships you have, have had, wish you had, or never had?

3. Being with your real self, without hesitating or shying away from full immersion in your total pleasure and joy, what parts/moments/aspects do you celebrate about the people you know? With that same forthright, unflinching look, what troubles you in your friendships, family, romance, with children, including the absence of any of those kinds of relationships?

4. Some say their relationship, particularly a primary one, is "good enough." When does that become settling? Is it okay to settle?

5. If your relationships satisfy you, what defines them? If you are looking for a satisfying personal relationship, how do you imagine your life would be if you had what you think you want?

6. What do you not do that enhances the relationships you seek or have? What do you do or not do that interferes with having the relationship(s) that you desire? If you asked people whom you could trust, what they see as your way of making relationships go well, what would they tell you? If you asked those same people how you get in your own way, what might they say, especially if they were not worried about hurting you?

7. If you were writing a relationship inventory of the good things you bring to a primary/romantic relationship, friendship, family connection, and the things you do that are complicated, problematic, annoying, worrisome, what would be on those lists? If you choose not to write about this question, you might ask yourself why.

8. What are three things you could do, today, that would expand the possibility of your having a new, close, personal, deep relationship if that is something you want? What three things could you do to create or improve your relationship, even if it is already good?

9. What can you celebrate that you do or don't do that makes you a fantastic partner/friend/family member? What can you celebrate that the other person/people do or don't do that makes that person a fantastic partner?

10. Let's get real. Are you the kind of partner you would like to have? How so? Let's get real. Is your partner really the kind of partner who is good and right for you?

11. You want to meet someone. How do you decide that they are good for you?

12. You are with someone, in romance or friendship. How do you assess that you are bringing your best self to the relationship? How do you assess that person is bringing their best self to the relationship?

13. One behavior that many partners demonstrate is called the summarizing self-syndrome. They keep telling their partner what the partner needs to do. The partner does not do it. This goes on for years. What are alternatives besides continuing to educate the other person on how they need to be?

14. One behavior that many people who want to be in a relationship do is to keep doing the same thing over and over to meet and develop relationships. Think about someone who was where you are and now is with someone. Besides luck, what did they do that could inform your choices?

15. What is your dream for a relationship? Are you living that dream? Do you offer that dream? Now what?

CHILDREN AND PETS

There are active choices, and there are passive choices. Saying yes or no to having a child or children can be an active choice, a chance decision, a passive decision, or a default experience, that is, just what happens. Most adults choose to have a child, and some adults are childless. What this means to your life cannot be overstated. Many lives revolve around children. For some people, their pet(s) fulfill the same, or some would say, a similar role as a child might or does. Pets are frequently considered family members with their own needs and wishes. Children and pets are major parts of many adults' lives. None of this is a surprise or particularly revealing to explore. What is important is how this active or passive choice creates or alters an individual's life. Having a pet surely matters to most people who have them and is in its distinct category of adding to a person's life.

Ask yourself each question offered. Consider responding to a question(s) that makes you smile, that you are attracted to answering, and to one or two you don't like or want to turn away from. Facing what you don't like, or are uncomfortable with, is often a path to the most significant learning. These questions are guides to prime or stimulate your memories and thoughts about your life. The questions are not intended to be answered in a literal manner. Read through each of them and react to the one(s) that open windows for you. Each life is unique, and the priming questions impact each of us differently.

SENSITIZING QUESTIONS AND PROMPTS

1. Growing up, was it your wish and plan to have children, or not? Where did that thought, plan, or assumption come from, and who contributed to that idea? Whether you have a child/children or not, how does that expectation fit you now?

2. Do you have children? How was the decision made to have them? How come? Who influenced the decision? What did your parents say or expect of you? Spoken or implied? If you had to work hard to have children due to whatever, what impact did that decision-making and process have on you?

3. Do you believe people who have children are better than people who do not? Do you have a judgment of childless people as selfish or less than you? If you are childless, do you have a judgment of people who have children? How does this difference impact your relationship with people in the opposite group who are important to you?

4. If you do not have children, was that by choice, chance, or default? Did you have to work hard to conceive and have a child? Were there medical reasons why you do not have children? When people ask you if you have children, what responses do your offer? What response do you imagine you will receive or have received from people who ask that questions? How have those responses felt to you?

5. Growing up, did you have a pet(s) who was a family member? What meaning, role, or function did that animal bring to you? Who was the animal's caretaker? What did you learn about life from having that critter be a part of your life, family? Was there a psychological connection, a bond, support, or a healing involvement with that being? Was there any trauma or pain associated with that animal in your family?

6. Do you have a pet now? Are they a family member, an animal, or even one that lives outside? Is there a way that an animal makes your life better, safer, more enriched, and feel more loved? Is there a way the animal is limiting, challenging, or seems to be a secondary substitute?

7. In your frame of reference, are animals and children similarly valuable, distinctly different, or both? How come? Do you consider yourself mainstream with this opinion or an "outlier"? Is that okay with you or not?

8. What do children bring into your life? What do children take from your life?

9. How has having children impacted your primary relationship(s) positively? In a negative way? What, if anything, do you need or want to do about changing the positive or negative reality of the children in your life?

10. As you look back, are you glad you had children or not? How would your life have been different if, as a person with children, you had not had a child or children? As you look back, are you glad you remained childless, by choice or any other way, or not? How would your life have been different if you had had children?

CONNECTIONS

The people, ideas, and experiences we have contribute to a full, rich, and good life. Identify those important people, those meaningful ideas or values, and the experiences of consequence in your life. Ask yourself the question — what is connection, and to whom am I connected? Connection is a point of contact, a moment or more, when we are with, become more aware of, the value of another person, idea, or experience. In these times when we are "with" the other, there is an aliveness that is necessary for the best life. Without it, and it is sometimes elusive, there is a longing to find it, in whatever form. In lives that are busy and demanding or lives that we fill with busyness and demands that may not be as important as we think they are, connections, while still needed, are often not noticed, not developed, not fostered, and, sometimes, not there. What to do, if anything?

Take time now and recall, savor, plan and just notice where those connections are, might be, have been, could be, would be wonderful to have with people, ideas, and experiences that are outside of you, that involves more than only you. There are risks in doing this exploration. You might get carried away with remembering what was glorious and what wasn't. You might find that you missed seeing what was there when it was. We all take things for granted and then wish we could have one more moment with that important person, that profoundly touching moment, or the sheer excitement of learning and getting a new insight or perspective on experiences outside of us. We don't always notice. Take time and notice — the connections that were, are, can be, and you want to develop.

For some people, there are automatic and positive connections available. That could be a supportive and encouraging family of origin, a sibling, a childhood friend, a partner, a powerful belief system that helps organize your way of being in life, a purpose that defines you, or an experience that makes it clear to you where you belong in this life. For others, none of that exists. And, of course, there is every experience in between.

Ask yourself each question offered. Consider responding to a question(s) that makes you smile, that you are attracted to answering, and to one or two you don't like or want to turn away from. Facing what you don't like, or are uncomfortable with, is often a path to the most significant learning. These questions are guides to prime or stimulate your memories and thoughts about your life. The questions are not intended to be answered in a literal manner. Read through each of them and react to the one(s) that open windows for you. Each life is unique, and the priming questions impact each of us differently.

SENSITIZING QUESTIONS AND PROMPTS

1. What does connection mean to you? What do you imagine are the ideal connections you or anyone might have? What do you imagine or experience that makes you feel that you have what you want or don't have what you want?

2. Can you list the connections to people, ideas, values, and experiences you have had in your life? Just make a list with no reflection or judgment.

3. Are connections important? How come? If not, why not?

4. Some would say that being connected, however that is, is always good. Some would say that connections can be good or not so good. What is your belief? When might they be a good thing? And then, again, when are they limiting or self-defeating even?

5. If you are honest with yourself and take stock, are there ways that the connections you have or have had that limit you? Do you invest too much in others? Do you acquiesce and give up on yourself to be what others want and need you to be? How does that serve you? How does that get in the way of your being the person you want to be?

6. If you say, "life would be just the way I want and need it to be to feel good, great, satisfied . . ." if I . . .?

7. In the past, in the earliest days of your life, did you feel connected to your family, a neighbor, a scout leader, a religious leader, a friend or two, a goal or focus, or something else? What did that give you that made your life better? If you still have those connections, how have you maintained them over the years? If they are lost to you, now, what happened? How is it to think about that?

8. Do you wonder about going back and doing some repair, healing, or exploration? What life lessons did you learn from those connections, whether ongoing or not, that serve you now?

9. Did you appreciate the connections you had at the time, or are they more valuable retrospectively? What did you miss, and how come you missed it? What got in the way of valuing what you had — be that a person, an idea, a value, an experience? Is there something to learn from what you did or didn't do then that might help you in your current life?

10. When one is disconnected or going through the motions of being present for their life, that disconnection can be out of one's awareness. It may seem counterintuitive that we may or may not be connected when there are many people around. Having people around does not mean that something real and worthwhile is going on. Are you connected or disconnected from the people in your world? How do you know? How do you define that? Do they know you? Is that okay? What does knowing you mean? Do you let them know you? Do you want them to know you? How come?

11. When one is connected to others, sometimes that is truly wonderful. Is that so for you? When one is connected to others, it can be a mixed bag. What works and what doesn't for you?

12. Do you need more connections? How might you go about expanding and/or enhancing connections in your life? What would you be seeking? What would be good to avoid? What connections are enervating (taking energy away from you) vs. connections that are energizing (bringing energy to you)?

13. What about experiences? Do you choose them, or do they choose you? Are your needs being met? Are you living too small? Are you living large in a "choice-full" way?

14. Then there are ideas. Do you seek stimulation for ideas, or are you so weary by the end of your day that you just survive without thinking about what would give you the life you want, a life of connection to the ideas and values that are important to you? If you are seeking ideas, do you bring them into an active part of your life? If not, how could you do that?

15. Are you connected to the world — people, ideas, experiences, values, and whatever else you care about — in the ways that give you the feelings you desire? If so, how can you maintain that way of life? If not, what is next for you?

FRIENDSHIPS: THE SWEETNESS AND THE PAIN

Friends have the potential to powerfully impact who we are and what kind of life we live. We have had friendships that have a greater effect on us than our families. We choose our friends actively and passively, consciously and unconsciously. Proximity, shared positive and difficult experiences, being like-minded, attraction, and affinity, help foster the development of an association, which becomes a friendship. Friendships usually do not have the obligatory aspect of family relationships. Friends can be acquaintances with whom you have a brief connection or a longtime confidant who accepts you fully, with many other variations.

According to Wikipedia, a friendship is a relationship of mutual affection between two or more people, a stronger form of interpersonal bond from an association. Research tells us that people with close friendships are happier. When we are fortunate, the characteristics that occur within a friendship include affection, empathy, honesty, altruism, mutual understanding and compassion, enjoyment of each other's company, trust, and the ability to be oneself, express one's feelings, and make mistakes without fear of judgment from that person. Sometimes, though, friendships develop serious limitations, disappointments, hurts, and let-down feelings that are poignant and painful after the closeness that was the core of the previous relationship. So perhaps it is inevitable that friendships will be tested, as is true in all types of relationships.

Perhaps there are inevitable differences that occur. However, how each person deals with those moments determines the friendship's depth, quality, meaning, and duration. For example, different expectations, changing needs, and increased awareness of what one wants from the friend all impact a friendship. Additionally, changing demographics such as getting married, becoming single, losing a job, moving to a new city, or receiving a scary medical diagnosis can alter the friendship's nature, safety, and desirability.

Ask yourself each question offered. Consider responding to a question(s) that makes you smile, that you are attracted to answering, and to one or two you don't like or want to turn away from. Facing what you don't like, or are uncomfortable with, is often a path to the most significant learning. These questions are guides to prime or stimulate your memories and thoughts about your life. The questions are not intended to be answered in a literal manner. Read through each of them and react to the one(s) that open windows for you. Each life is unique, and the priming questions impact each of us differently.

SENSITIZING QUESTIONS AND PROMPTS

1. In your mind and heart, what essential elements are required to call someone a friend? What are the essential elements necessary to be a friend?

2. What do you want most from your friendships? What do you like to offer to people you have or might have a friendship with?

3. Have you had a "best" friend? Do you now? Did you ever fight with that person? What happened? Did you resolve it? How did that happen?

4. With that best friend, what started the relationship, kept it going, or ended it if it is not ongoing? When you think of that person and the experience of that relationship, how do you define it, and hold it in your thoughts?

5. Have you lost a good friend through death, moving away, or discord? How did you handle the loss? What thoughts do you have about that relationship now?

6. Are you a good friend? What makes that so?

7. Describe what friendship means to you. Have you had what you want from and with other people?

8. What are three things about yourself you have learned from the friendships you have had?

9. Did your parents support the friends you chose? What did they like? What didn't they like? Did that make the person you wanted as a friend more or less valuable to you? What did you do? What do you now think about their ideas of what was right for you?

10. Have you had sweetness, pain in your friendships, or both? What did you do to contribute to the relationship flourishing or floundering? Do you talk directly about concerns, hope the issue will go away, or something else?

11. IF you have suffered in your friendships, what do you do now to select new people to bring into life and have confidence that the relationship will likely be good for you?

12. What are warning signs that someone is not a good choice to have as a friend? What do you do when you see those signs? For example, this new person in your life only talks about themselves. What do you do or say, if anything?

13. Can people who are sexually attracted to each other be friends? Is it good to talk about the attraction or not? What are the parameters that make sense to you?

14. If you were writing a legacy of the friends who have had the most meaning in your life — positive or negative — who are they, and what did they bring to you?

15. Have your friends changed over the years? Was there a time when a friend helped you out that you will never forget?

16. Can you be friends with family members, or, by definition, are they always family members? Can you have a friendship with your adult child?

17. Can you be friends with your partner/spouse? Do you require more from a partner than from a friend? Do you need more from your friend than you do from a partner? Is that okay with you as you think about it now?

18. What would you consider to be a relationship breach? Has that happened to you? Were you the person who breached the relationship, or were you the recipient of someone else's poor behavior? What do you take away from that situation?

19. Can you outgrow your friendships? Has that happened? How are you about that now?

20. Have you had a fair-weather friend? Have you had a friend who only was interested in you if you were upbeat/happy or was only there if you were suffering/miserable? What does that mean to you?

21. As you review your friendships, is there anyone (or more than one) with whom you would like to have contact now? What would you say to them? What would you want them to know? Will you take this action and contact them? If so, do you have any concerns or trepidations? Is there timeliness to your intention to be in touch?

22. Do you have any friends you would like to have met each other, whether or not that is possible? How come?

23. Has your life been enriched by friends or are you primarily disappointed in how those relationships have gone over time? Are you somewhere in between those two ends of the continuum?

24. What do you want or need by way of friendships now? How will you find what you need? How will you assess if what you are doing is good and right for you or not?

25. Do you need to weed out some people you have thought of as friends, but they just need to go? Why? Will you let them go? Will you talk to them about your decision? Will you just be too busy to see them?

26. If a friend has "wronged" you, will you talk to them about your hurts, disappointments, anger, or not? How come?

27. There is often a person with whom you really, really want a friendship. Still, there is some obstacle — perhaps you don't like their partner, maybe you feel less than and do not think they would want to be your friend, maybe they have more education/money/experiences/fitness, etc. than you do. What do you do about that? Do you shy away? Do you go toward? Do you talk about your differences? Do you focus on where the connection is?

28. Are your friends similar or different from you? Do you have to share the same moral values to be good friends? Do you have to share the same political viewpoints or religious beliefs to be good friends?

29. What are your needs, or do you want to have met in your friendships? Do you want support, a community, a social life, a go-to person, or something else?

30. How do you find friends? Where do you go? What do you do? What do you avoid doing, like staying in your house hoping the good ones will find you?

31. Is there a moment when you just know that this person you have spent time with is good and right for you? Do you acknowledge that at the moment? Do you wait and see if it will last? Do you trust the experience? Do you doubt the experience?

32. In reflecting on "friendship," what is most important to you now?

PERSONAL BOUNDARIES: WHERE, WHEN, AND HOW TO DRAW THE LINE?

Ida Soghomonian tells us, "Personal boundaries are guidelines, rules or limits that a person creates to identify reasonable, safe and permissible ways for other people to behave towards them and how they will respond when someone exceeds those limits." Whether they are conscious and known or unconscious, they exist within us. Sometimes, though, for a variety of reasons, we ignore, deny, deflect, seem to "forget" or fail to follow through on the personal boundaries we know we need. Personal boundaries include things, space, thoughts, emotions, and physical or sexual limits.

It may be hard to set boundaries because you put others' needs and feelings first; you don't know yourself, what you want and need; you don't feel you have the right to say what you want and have what you want; you believe and fear setting boundaries jeopardizes the relationship and you may be right, and you never learned to have healthy boundaries. Boundaries are learned. If, for example, you weren't valued as a child, you didn't learn that you could have and express boundaries. Any kind of abuse violates personal boundaries.

Many people grow up learning to please, accommodate, and care for others. That is a primary role for many females. Women who grew up in the 1950s, 1960s, 1970s, and 1980s learned that being a certain way would frequently get them the rewards they wanted. Some parents developed primary attachments to their children rather than their partner, and the child's job of partnering with the parent had status and an elevated role. The downside to that experience was the child who was the parent's partner did not get to do their own exploring and growing as a child, rather than as the pseudo-adult they were being asked/required/demanded to be. The role could be very seductive. Then, there is the child who pleased to get anything good from parents who were distracted, distressed, absent for whatever reason—work, health, other obligations, or lack of interest in being a parent.

Many other scenarios, too, taught that personal boundaries were not okay. The fortunate child is the one who was told to take care of themselves, speak up, say what s/he needed, and even when s/he could not have what was being requested, that child was encouraged, not shamed, for having preferences, needs, and wishes.

Ask yourself each question offered. Consider responding to a question(s) that makes you smile, that you are attracted to answering, and to one or two you don't like or want to turn away from. Facing what you don't like, or are uncomfortable with, is often a path to the most significant learning. These questions are guides to prime or stimulate your memories and thoughts about your life. The questions are not intended to be answered in a literal manner. Read through each of them and react to the one(s) that open windows for you. Each life is unique, and the priming questions impact each of us differently.

SENSITIZING QUESTIONS AND PROMPTS

1. How often do you say "yes" when you want to say "no"? Or do you not answer, give a vague response to allow for some wiggle room when you want to say "no"? Do you have another way to avoid saying "no"?

2. What would be included if you were to write a personal bill of rights for yourself, clearly outlining your boundaries for each situation and person in your life? Would you assert those rights you outlined for yourself? If not, how come? If so, would you be concerned or worried about any particular response(s) you might get?

3. What are the statements that describe your bottom line in relationships? For example, "Please don't criticize me" or "Please only say positive things to me about me or don't say anything at all." Or "Thank you for thinking of me, but I won't be joining/helping you/doing x for you."

4. With whom or in what situations do you have the easiest time setting personal boundaries? Why do you think those situations or people are more manageable for you? What can you learn from that awareness?

5. With whom or in what situations do you have the most difficulty setting personal boundaries? Why do you think those situations or people are more challenging for you? What can you learn from that awareness?

6. Do you know anyone who sets clear and firm personal boundaries in a way you respect and appreciate? Who is that person or those people? What is it like for you to be the recipient of that person's limit setting? Are there times when you want that and others when you are uncomfortable or dislike being the recipient of that person's choices?

7. What can you recall of the boundaries of your parents or caregivers? Were they clear with what was okay and what was not? How was that for you?

8. What did you learn from your caregivers about what was okay for you to do? For example, was it all right for you to say "no" to a request from your parent/caregiver? Did your parents expect you, require you, to do whatever they wanted, or was there a high and adverse price to pay? How was that for you? What lingering feelings, if any, do you have about those relationships because of their expectations for you?

9. As a parent or caregiver of others, do you allow your children to set boundaries? Can you respect and honor them even if you dislike their limit? Or do you get angry and rejecting if that child does not do what you want them to do?

10. In a close friendship, can and do you say "yes" or "no" depending on what you want? Do you think about what is better for you when committing to, agreeing to, or even offering something to another?

11. Has there been a time when, in retrospect, you know you gave up on yourself and accommodated/acquiesced with resentment to another person's needs? Do you have lingering feelings about your decision? If you revisit that time now, what do you see that you brought to that choice point from your past, and what do you take forward, so you take better care of yourself in the future?

12. Do you feel resentful or victimized in any current or past relationship? Who and what is your feeling or experience? Did you or do you set the boundaries necessary to care of yourself with that person? Anger often is a signal that action is required. What would be the good and right thing to do to fix that situation, whether you intend to take that action or not? If you want to act, when and what will you do? What are the exact words you might use to communicate now what you need? If you do not intend to take action, what stops you? Is that okay with you? What would it take to move you toward taking the action (s) you want and need to take?

13. Sometimes we say, "I did set the boundary, but it didn't work!" Perhaps there is a better way to set the limit. Think about how you could do it better the next time. If you say the other person will not hear me, then what? What is it you can do, without their agreement, to take care of yourself? For example, if you say to someone, "Please speak to me in a kind way using a soft voice." They then yell at you or put you down. You can repeat it one more time. The following statement could be, "If you talk to me this way again, I'll need to leave." If they talk to you that way, again, you must leave if you said you would. Could you do that in the situation you are imagining? If not, is their treatment of you something you can live with forever since that is what you are agreeing to do?

14. Is there someone in your life who uses boundaries as a punishment? That is, they will not love you or show up for you if you don't do something they want. Is that love?

15. Can all boundaries be negotiated? What personal boundaries are non-negotiable for you?

16. What is one new boundary you have either neglected or just thought about now that you want to add to your life? How hard will it be for you to add in this new limit for yourself? How will you remind yourself of this plan for yourself? How can you make it more doable for you?

17. If you are asked to do or not do something, are you required to respond right away or could you let yourself say, "Let me think about that," and then think about your boundary, returning to the person who asked with your reply?

18. If you were going to teach someone you care about—a partner, a child, a close friend—about the value of personal boundaries, what is the one clear message you would like to offer? Write it out clearly. Is that a message for a particular person? Is that also a message for you?

HEROES OR HEROINES AND VILLAINS

A hero or heroine a person who is admired for courage or noble qualities. A villain is a person guilty or capable of a crime or wickedness. Life is impacted by those people we encounter at home, school, work, wherever we go, and whatever we do. They teach directly and indirectly. Sometimes they encourage us to move toward a way of being. Other times they teach us to move away from something. The heroes or heroines and the villains we encounter are important in many ways. They have the potential to alter our lives forever. We may be a hero or heroine or villain to others, too. It matters to notice when we know, think, or feel we are bringing that self, that way of being, to someone else.

Ask yourself each question offered. Consider responding to a question(s) that makes you smile, that you are attracted to answering, and to one or two you don't like or want to turn away from. Facing what you don't like, or are uncomfortable with, is often a path to the most significant learning. These questions are guides to prime or stimulate your memories and thoughts about your life. The questions are not intended to be answered in a literal manner. Read through each of them and react to the one(s) that open windows for you. Each life is unique, and the priming questions impact each of us differently.

SENSITIZING QUESTIONS AND PROMPTS

1. What is a hero or heroine and a villain?
2. Have any people played either role in your life?
3. Was that a hero, heroine, villain, or perhaps both?
4. What did you take from that experience, that relationship, be it for a moment or a lifetime?
5. Have you told the person? Do you want to tell them? Why? What would you say?
6. If you had more of one than the other, can you imagine why?
7. Were you a hero, heroine, or villain in someone else's life? How do you know?
8. Do you want to be a hero or heroine to someone now, and if so, to whom?
9. Why does that matter to you? How would you start?
10. What is the legacy of being a hero or villain?
11. How would your life be different if you had not had the experience you did with that particular hero or villain?
12. What is the best thing about having a villain in your life? And the worst?
13. What is the best thing about having a hero or heroine in your life? And the worst?
14. Does a hero, heroine, or villain have to be someone you know or knew? Can that person be real but not in your actual world, imagined, from history, alive or dead?
15. Does everyone need a hero or heroine or a villain? Does everyone have a hero or heroine?

16. If you wanted to be in either role to someone else, now, to whom and what would you bring?

17. Is there someone you want to invite into your life as a hero, heroine, or villain? (Keep your friends close. Keep your enemies closer.)

18. Is a villain an enemy? Is a hero or heroine always good?

19. Have you categorized people as heroes, heroines, or villains before? Does it give you clarity? Does it provide you with something else? Is it limiting in some way?

ROMANCE: WHO WERE/ARE THEY, THOSE ROMANTIC PEOPLE IN YOUR LIFE

Many of us want romantic relationships. Few among us prefer to be alone. Being emotionally and physically close to another person is a deep need, so profound that many of us cannot live without becoming romantically involved with others. And yet, intimate relationships are complicated. Think about your hopes and dreams for your connection with others. Notice where you have fulfilled those wishes and where there are ongoing or new desires, and longings.

Ask yourself each question offered. Consider responding to a question(s) that makes you smile, that you are attracted to answering, and to one or two you don't like or want to turn away from. Facing what you don't like, or are uncomfortable with, is often a path to the most significant learning. These questions are guides to prime or stimulate your memories and thoughts about your life. The questions are not intended to be answered in a literal manner. Read through each of them and react to the one(s) that open windows for you. Each life is unique, and the priming questions impact each of us differently.

SENSITIZING QUESTIONS AND PROMPTS

1. What is a romantic relationship? Do you have an excellent romantic relationship(s) with anyone? How do you know? What do the people around you say about your relationship with them? What do you tell yourself about the intimate relationships you have — be they intensely romantic, casual, intense, hoped for, whatever kind?

2. Do you define yourself by the relationships you have or have had or wish you had, or never had?

3. Being with your authentic self, without hesitating or shying away from complete immersion in your total pleasure and joy, what parts/moments/aspects do you celebrate about the people you know? With that same forthright, unflinching look, what troubles you in your romantic life, including the absence of any of those relationships, now or in the past?

4. Many say their relationship, particularly a primary one, is "good enough." When does that become settling? Is it okay to settle?

5. If you have relationships that satisfy you, what defines them? If you are looking for a satisfying romantic relationship, how do you imagine your life would be if you had what you think you want?

6. What do you not do that enhances the relationships you seek or have? What do you do or not do that interferes with your having the relationship(s) that you desire? If you asked people whom you could trust, what they see as your way of making relationships go well, what would they tell you? If you asked those same people how you get in your way, what might they say, especially if they were not worried about hurting you?

7. If you were going to do a relationship inventory of what good things you bring to a primary/romantic relationship and what things you do that are complicated, problematic, annoying, or worrisome, what would be on those lists? If you choose not to write about this question, you might ask yourself why.

8. What are three things you could do today that would expand the possibility of your having a new, close, personal, deep relationship if that is something you want? What are three things you could do, beginning today, to create or improve your relationship, even if they are already good?

9. What can you celebrate that you do or don't do that makes you a fantastic partner? What can you observe that the other person/people do or don't do that makes that person a fantastic partner?

10. Let's get real. Are you the kind of partner you would like to have? How so? Let's get real. Is your partner the kind of partner who is good and right for you?

11. You want to meet someone. How do you assess that they are good for you?

12. You are with someone in a romance. How do you judge whether you bring your best self to the relationship? How do you test that partners bring their best selves to the relationship?

13. One behavior that many partners demonstrate is called summarizing self-syndrome. They keep telling their partner what the partner needs to do. The partner does not do it. This goes on for years. What are alternatives besides continuing to educate the other person on how they need to be?

14. One behavior that many people who want to be in a relationship do is repeating the same thing over and over to meet and develop relationships. Think about someone who was where you are and now is with someone. Besides luck, what did they do that could inform your choices?

15. What is your dream for a romantic relationship? Do you have it?

16. Naturally, where romance is concerned, many parts of you will be necessary to explore. What else comes to you that you believe would help you to be in a successful romantic connection?

CATEGORY V

HEALTH AND WELL-BEING

Physical Health

Your Body – Your Sexual Self

Your Mental Health

Our physical, sexual, and psychological selves are central to our well-being. What you can and cannot do and what you believe you can and cannot do often direct you to one kind of life. We each have ideas, beliefs, and experiences of these aspects of our being. Some of us believe everything is given and will remain that way. Others believe anything is possible. Our ideas—beliefs, thoughts, feelings—about our health and well-being direct much of our lives. Seeing what your stories are about your body, what you saw and learned, what your health profile became, and whether you are lucky or not, your genetics make a difference. Health, energy, strength/weakness, vulnerability, and vitality is central to every experience we have, every story we live, and every aspect of our being. What do you think about your health and well-being?

PHYSICAL HEALTH

Good health matters. Sometimes our health is good, and sometimes our health is not so good. That is true for the people around us and those we care for and about. Good health can mean we have many options. Moderate, poor, or declining health limits those options. Everyone gets something sooner or later. Everyone struggles with their health at some time. Some people struggle more. Some people struggle at a younger age than they imagined. Some people struggle less. We are fortunate if we can face the day with energy, enthusiasm, and a sense of well-being. Health affects everything.

We can do some things to improve and maintain our health. Sometimes, though, we get what we get. Many important things are said about health. Our health and the health of the people we care for matter. It is fundamental. It is critical. It is significant. Some people take their health for granted even if they know better. Some people are more vigilant and active in caring for and maintaining their health. Like other parts of life, we cannot think about health every minute, or there would be no life. The meaning of health and well-being in your life shapes what you do and don't do, can do, and cannot do, with whom you interact, how you view yourself, and so much more.

There are less or more challenging phases if you are a caregiver of others, professionally and personally, as well as a caring for your own health. There are thoughts, behaviors, feelings, and sensations as we experience our health and the health of people around us. There may be judgments we make. There may be beliefs. There may be science we depend on to clarify our experience with health. There may be the wisdom of the ages we turn to determine our relationship with health. Collecting our ideas and responses can profoundly impact our healthful or unhealthful life.

While we each have a physical body, how we live in it and with it has many variations. Whether our relationship with our body is conscious, unconscious, or both makes a difference. What we do or don't do with it, how we tend to it or not, and how we think about it or don't have enormous consequences. Your body can be a pal to which you are loyal or a foe which you prefer to ignore, and everywhere in between. Body health and well-being can relate to physical, sensual, sexual, psychological, and spiritual health. We have expectations, judgments, and responses to our own and other people's bodies and health. Others respond to our bodies, health, and well-being, too. The reality of your relationship with your body and health has a significant impact on the choices you make. Take stock, pause, and reflect. What is there to notice?

Ask yourself each question offered. Consider responding to a question(s) that makes you smile, that you are attracted to answering, and to one or two you don't like or want to turn away from. Facing what you don't like, or are uncomfortable with, is often a path to the most significant learning. These questions are guides to prime or stimulate your memories and thoughts about your life. The questions are not intended to be answered in a literal manner. Read through each of them and react to the one(s) that open windows for you. Each life is unique, and the priming questions impact each of us differently.

SENSITIZING QUESTIONS AND PROMPTS

1. Can you impact your health? How much of a role do genetics play?

2. If you can impact your health with your choices, do you do what you must do? If yes, how come? If not, why not? Do you have judgments about what other people whom you care for or care about do or do not do? How do you handle those judgments either directly or indirectly?

3. If someone you care about takes care of their health, do you feel better about them? If someone you care about takes poor care, limited care, or doesn't take care of their health, do you think less of them or have other feelings — negative, compassionate, protective, angry, etc.? Do you tell them? If yes, how does that go? If not, why not

4. If you look at your health over your lifetime, how would you describe it? Generally healthy? Frequently challenged? Seriously compromised? What does that mean to you?

5. What do you notice if you reflect on your health at each stage of life—childhood, adolescence, adulthood?

6. What are the implications of aging for you and the people you love? Are there some people for whom the changes mainly concern you? Who are they? Are you doing what you want and need to do as you reflect on those concerns? If not, for whom do you want to reconsider your behavior? Do you want or need to have conversations with them? How would you start?

7. Disability, short-term or long term is a worry for many people. Many of us have thoughts about what we would want or not want and who would be there for us or not. Is this an area of your life that needs attention and conversation with people around you? Will you have those discussions?

8. Addictions and substance abuse are a significant struggle for many people and their families. What role have they played in your life or those around you? What are your concerns or fears that need your attention, if any?

9. Some people are aggressive about tending to their health, wanting to explore and discover whatever they might about their health. Other people are more passive and feel better letting come what comes. Where are you on that spectrum? Was that right for you in the past? Is that right for you now? Is that right for the people you care about and who care about you?

10. Anything you might want to do differently now?

YOUR BODY – YOUR SEXUAL SELF

Our bodies serve us in myriad ways—movement, choices, pleasure, and the inevitable health challenges, pain, and loss over time. Caring for and about your body when it is healthy and does not need a lot has its possibilities; tending to your body when the needs are more complicated, challenging, and distressing is its own process. Seeing yourself as a sensual and sexual person with all the options that implies is wonderful for some people and confusing or not of any interest to others. Where you are on that continuum undoubtedly impacts many life decisions. Your personal history, relationship with yourself and others, and possibilities, influence this meaningful part of life.

Ask yourself each question offered. Consider responding to a question(s) that makes you smile, that you are attracted to answering, and to one or two you don't like or want to turn away from. Facing what you don't like, or are uncomfortable with, is often a path to the most significant learning. These questions are guides to prime or stimulate your memories and thoughts about your life. The questions are not intended to be answered in a literal manner. Read through each of them and react to the one(s) that open windows for you. Each life is unique, and the priming questions impact each of us differently.

SENSITIZING QUESTIONS AND PROMPTS

1. What do you think of as your body? Is it simply physical, or is it also emotional and psychological, spiritual, sensual, and sexual?

2. What are five words you would use to describe your body? Are those words from inside you, or are they learned from someone else? Whose voice do you hear in those words? Are they positive, negative, neutral, descriptive, or judgmental?

3. What part(s) of your body do you value the most? The least? If there are parts of your body with which you are not comfortable, how does that influence your overall feelings about yourself? Does this area of your being need attention to appreciate what you do have?

4. How do you care for your body if you do? If you don't?

5. What is your most positive or pleasurable body experience?

6. What was or is your most problematic body experience?

7. How would you describe your body to someone you were willing to be vulnerable with if you were telling them about your body? How does that sound to you? Many people are highly critical of their bodies. If that is true for you, is this something to explore and possibly heal?

8. Are all bodies sensual? Sexual? If you are in touch with your sexual self, are you having a positive experience now? A negative experience? Is that okay with you if you are not in touch with your sexual self now? How come? Do you consider yourself a sexual being? If so, is the expression of your

sexual self what you feel you want and need? If yes, is that complete for now? If not, are there steps you are willing to explore or take to feel more of what you want?

9. What are the first positive things you notice about your body?

10. Do you look at your body? Do you see your body? Do you like what you see today? Can you let yourself see something positive about your body if that is not what you see at first look? If you were to make some change to your body now, what would be a modest step that could last a lifetime?

11. Do you have a "type" or preference for the body of the person you are attracted to? What is physically unattractive to you in another person? How is that for you to say, think, notice, and comment on?

12. If someone else described your body as . . . (fill in the blank), would you feel good, bad, indifferent, something else?

13. What words would describe your relationship with your body e.g., relaxed, at war, thrilled, detached, etc.?

14. Are you loyal to your body? Or disloyal?

15. Does presenting your body in specific ways have meaning for you? What are those ways? Are you meeting your challenge?

16. What would you see if you look at photographs of your body from when you were two years old, 12, 22, 32, 42, 52, 62, 72, 82, or 92 years old? What would you hope to see if you have not yet reached that number? Many people were told, growing up, that their body was not okay in some way. If that was true for you, has that left scars, worries, or pain? Do you need to heal that pain now? How has that negative perception impacted your expression of your sexual self?

17. What is your secret, or perhaps not so secret, thought about your body?

18. If you had a banner across your chest proclaiming what your body would say if it could speak, what would that banner read?

19. If you could take a pill tonight and have the body you want tomorrow, would it be the same or different than the body you have? How so?

20. If you are interested in a sexual life, do you have what you want? If you do, are there changes that would make it even better? Will you attend to making that part of your life better, or not?

21. If you do not have what you want, are you interested in exploring how to have more of the experiences or feelings you are interested in?

22. Are the rules for being a sexual person different as you age? What changes would you be interested in making?

23. Can someone your current age have a romantic relationship with their current partner? A new partner? Do you want a romantic relationship? Do you want a sexual relationship? Will you seek out what you want or make some assumptions that you can't have that because of something?

24. Sensuality, sexuality, and sex are on a continuum involving many factors. Is this an essential part of your life or something of no interest, minimal interest, fear, or something else that keeps you from looking at this aspect of life? Is that okay with you? If not, how can you move forward, even if that means considering options, talking to a friend or therapist, or taking other definitive, explicit actions to open up this part of your life?

YOUR MENTAL HEALTH

While all the themes we discuss in this book relate to your mental health, your specific look at your well-being and sense of yourself is focused on here. Considering life choices, noticing what is good and positive in your life, forgiveness for what you have or have not done (freeing brain space), and compassion for yourself and others make for a better, if not easier, life. Review, reflection, reconsideration, and renewal are paths forward, but looking back, taking stock, and noticing what matters can give you clarity and energy to see what is ahead or create a new way forward.

Ask yourself each question offered. Consider responding to a question(s) that makes you smile, that you are attracted to answering, and to one or two you don't like or want to turn away from. Facing what you don't like, or are uncomfortable with, is often a path to the most significant learning. These questions are guides to prime or stimulate your memories and thoughts about your life. The questions are not intended to be answered in a literal manner. Read through each of them and react to the one(s) that open windows for you. Each life is unique, and the priming questions impact each of us differently.

SENSITIZING QUESTIONS AND PROMPTS

1. What does well-being mean for you? For others around you?

2. What does the mind-body connection mean to you? Do they both matter? Does one matter more? Should it? Does one need more attention?

3. Since few of us make good choices all the time, how have you tended to your body and mind in the past? Now?

4. What does that mean if you have experienced serious mental and physical health challenges? How has that changed you? If it hasn't, what do you make of that when you think about it now?

5. If your challenge has been around your mental health, if you take stock now, how did you handle it? How are you handling it now?

6. Are there people around you who help, contribute, and improve your life and well-being? Do they know their value in your life?

7. Are people around you who take away value and pleasure from your life? Do you speak up about what works and what doesn't? Do you stay silent? How come? Is there a small change that would be helpful to make? Can you let them go from your life?

8. Is addiction a part of your life, now or in the past? Being addicted is frequently a way to avoid feelings. Are you addicted to something in the past, or now? Alcohol? Drugs? Sex? Money? Being too busy? Being too what? Too much of too much can be a way to avoid your life. Is that true for you in any way? Is that true for the people closest to you?

9.   What is your goal, if you have one, about well-being? Are you moving toward it? Do you have language for what well-being means to you?

10. Now what? What is next for you regarding your well-being? How will you get there? How will you remember?

CATEGORY VI

TRANSITIONS

Living Alone

Limits. Loss

Grief

Shifts or changes big and small, momentary, or ongoing, chosen or not, impact each of us. If the change you are experiencing is something you desire or want, that is very different than if the transition is someone else's choice. Also, your responses are likely different if the change is by chance or default. Transitions, even small ones, impact some people more than others. As you imagine the tiny to immense shifts you have been through and those you anticipate, take note of your ease or dread, or whatever is in between, to get a reading of your resilience. Depending on the context of the transition and if more than one thing is happening simultaneously, your response will be distinct. Changes can, and often do, define us. Sometimes that is a positive vector, and then again, maybe not. Having a name for what is happening, a transition can make it more manageable, something everyone must address. That might help. We all have transitions to experience. What are your stories?

LIVING ALONE

Living alone is its own experience; some of us dread the idea, are fearful of all sorts of things, and do almost anything to keep it from happening. Other people relish their time living alone, seek it, require it, and savor it. Whatever your predisposition, most of us will have some time living alone, by choice, chance, or default. Of course, the reason or circumstance that has you living alone makes a huge difference in what that is like for you. If you are an introvert, your experience of living alone will obviously and clearly be quite different from the extroverted person. If there is a pandemic, a sudden announcement from a partner that they are leaving, a health crisis, and suddenly everything changes, that will impact the experience. While the specifics of who you are and how living alone came to be is worth taking note of, for many aging people, their worst fear is what life will be like, or is like, when a long-term partner is gone.

Ask yourself each question offered. Consider responding to a question(s) that makes you smile, that you are attracted to answering, and to one or two you don't like or want to turn away from. Facing what you don't like, or are uncomfortable with, is often a path to the most significant learning. These questions are guides to prime or stimulate your memories and thoughts about your life. The questions are not intended to be answered in a literal manner. Read through each of them and react to the one(s) that open windows for you. Each life is unique, and the priming questions impact each of us differently.

SENSITIZING QUESTIONS AND PROMPTS.

1. If you have never lived alone, how come? Are you curious about the possibility, want to avoid the idea, or somewhere in between?

2. While growing up, did you know people who lived alone? What did you imagine was happening in their lives? Did you find the idea of being on your own/living on your own appealing, or not? Were you drawn to the possibility, or did you find it sad or poignant, something else?

3. Can you prepare for a time when you live alone? Even with preparation, is it an unfolding that must be experienced?

4. Living alone means many different things. Some live with partners, children, grandchildren, siblings, friends, roommates, housemates, or caregivers. Considering the concept of living alone, what does that mean to you? Are some of those choices better for you to imagine than living in your space alone?

5. You might live in various circumstances at different times, feeling and being more alone. What is the best option you have or can imagine on a continuum? What is at the other end of the spectrum? How come?

6. As you sit in your life today, what are your thoughts, beliefs, ideas, and fears about living alone? What comes up immediately at the very idea? Pleasure? Pain? Fear? Relief? Terror? Peace?

7. As you tune into your own experience, can you imagine the opposite? If you are terrified at the idea of being on your own, living alone for an unknown amount of time, can you imagine the quiet being a good thing for you?

8. Are there specific things that living alone would, could, might bring you? How do you want where you live to be—neat, messy, cold, warm, whatever?

9. Are there specific things that living alone might bring that are distressing? What would you do if you didn't feel well emotionally or physically, found a giant spider in your bed or a rat in your home?

10. Will you do just about anything to live alone? Have you avoided committing to any relationship, so you don't have to share your space, your life? How come? In retrospect, was that a good decision? If so, how come? If not, why not? What is there to learn from the choices you have made?

11. Will you do just about anything not to live alone? Have you gotten into a relationship that might not have been so good for you to avoid being alone? Have you stayed in a problematic relationship to avoid being alone? How come? In retrospect, was that a good decision? If so, how come? If not, why not? What is there to learn from the choices you have made?

12. What do you notice about yourself if you are living alone for the first time? How is it different than you thought it would be, or the same? Can you imagine living alone for a long time, even for the rest of your life, or is this just a step along the way in your mind?

13. If you are living alone because of a sudden change not of your choosing—a health crisis, a breakup/divorce, something catastrophic happened, how are you faring? What has made this tolerable, if it is? What have you learned? What would you say to someone else you care for about how to take the first steps and what, if anything, helped you move into this time of your life while staying upright?

14. If you are living alone because of a sudden change of your choosing—what observations do you make about how you got there? Did you make this change in a timely way? In a thoughtful, choice-full way, impulsively? Is this change good and right for you? How do you feel about the other people or person involved—partner, children, or others? Did you say what you wanted and needed to say as you made this change? Do you have more to say to anyone involved? Will you tell the rest of what you have to say, now or in the future?

15. If you live with one person or more, do you have thoughts about what would be good, positive, and valuable if and when living alone? What are those thoughts? What are those plans? What might be helpful to do or consider or plan for now to help you when that time comes?

16. As you reflect on your life, who have you witnessed living alone and doing well? Looking back, who have you seen living alone and not doing well? What is there to learn from those observations? What is there to ask of someone living alone about how they handle whatever might be of importance for you to learn?

17. If you are not limited in your emotional or physical capacity or worry about what will happen if you do become dependent, do you know what might be helpful for you to consider doing, arranging, discussing, and exploring at this time? Whom might you speak with? What would you say?

18. What would comfort you if you took time to anticipate how life would be if you suddenly lived alone by chance, by choice, or by default?

LIMITS. LOSS

Every life has limits and loss of one kind or another. We each have to face things that are emotionally and physically challenging, scary, upsetting, or disappointing. As is true in so much of life, how we handle that limit or loss makes all the difference. After an accident or when something unexpected happens, we might say, "This isn't fair," "Why me," or "I cannot handle this," or "This cannot be true." The twins of loving and loss, that is, the inevitability that if you love, at some time, there will be loss, is something most of us do not want to face even though we know it.

Loss comes in all forms. Illness—short-term, acute, ongoing, chronic, debilitating, terminal. Loss of the previous healthy body. Disability. Separation. Divorce. Birth of a child with health concerns or the developing awareness of those over time. Job loss. Fires. Earthquakes. Just changing your mind. Each of us shall face loss.

Ask yourself each question offered. Consider responding to a question(s) that makes you smile, that you are attracted to answering, and to one or two you don't like or want to turn away from. Facing what you don't like, or are uncomfortable with, is often a path to the most significant learning. These questions are guides to prime or stimulate your memories and thoughts about your life. The questions are not intended to be answered in a literal manner. Read through each of them and react to the one(s) that open windows for you. Each life is unique, and the priming questions impact each of us differently.

SENSITIZING QUESTIONS AND PROMPTS

1. As a child, was there significant loss in your family, in yourself, or with other important people in your life? What happened? How did it, and does it affect you now?

2. As an adult, has there been significant loss in your family, in yourself, or with other important people in your life? What happened? How did it, and does it affect you now?

3. Have you experienced significant personal loss? What happened? If this is in the past, have the issues, concerns, and pain been resolved, or is there more to do? If this is current, what do you need? What are the questions that you are trying to answer for yourself? What kind of support or help would make this time better for you, help you grow, heal, or face the loss? Can you ask for what you need and let yourself receive what is offered?

4. What is next for you, even knowing there are limits? Are there limits or losses that are most frightening for you? Is there anything to do to help handle or mitigate those concerns?

5. As one ages, there are limits ahead. What are the limits in your sight now? How do you deal with those limits? Are you seeing them accurately, or do you amplify or diminish their reality? What are the consequences of these limits on your life, relationships, and planning?

6. If you have had significant tragedy in your life, how has that changed you, what have you learned about yourself, and what do you need? Would it help to write your story of what happened with whatever detail you choose to bring to that story? Is there repair or healing that you still need? From whom?

7. Are you someone who anticipates loss and plans for it, or are you the person who deals with things as they occur? On reflection, is what you do right, or do you need more of the other? What would that look like?

8. Does the awareness that there are limits and loss in every life activate you and get you going to do more of whatever is important to you, or is it enervating/taking your energy away so you don't do things because they will end? Is one more okay than the other?

9. What would you say to your children or a young person about limits and loss if you wanted them to face life with hope and good will?

10. Limits and loss are inevitable. How can hold that idea in a way that allows you to live your best life? Some say that if you live your life with the awareness of death, if you are not too freaked out about it, you live a better, more choice-full life. How would that awareness be for you?

GRIEF

Rabbis tell us that people believe they will live forever. None of us do. Grief and depression are different. Everyone experiences grief. There are the stages of grief that have been written about extensively. What is often overlooked is that people grieve on their own timetable, in their way, which is often different from the other people around them. There is no right or wrong way to grieve. We each find our way. The dictionary defines grief as deep and poignant distress. Listening, understanding, giving, and receiving emotional support are all helpful responses to grief, a naturally occurring part of each of our lives. No one is spared.

Ask yourself each question offered. Consider responding to a question(s) that makes you smile, that you are attracted to answering, and to one or two you don't like or want to turn away from. Facing what you don't like, or are uncomfortable with, is often a path to the most significant learning. These questions are guides to prime or stimulate your memories and thoughts about your life. The questions are not intended to be answered in a literal manner. Read through each of them and react to the one(s) that open windows for you. Each life is unique, and the priming questions impact each of us differently.

SENSITIZING QUESTIONS AND PROMPTS

1. What is your earliest experience of grief? How has it impacted your life? In your family, did people turn toward facing grief or mostly turn away from it by not talking about it?

2. What have been your personal experiences with the grief of whatever kind? Who helped you? Who didn't? What did that teach you about trusting others, helping others, and recovering from whatever the feelings were for you?

3. What help do you need when grieving? Do the people around you know what would support you or not? Have you told them? Do you want to tell them?

4. Do you have compassionate conversations about how you can/could be helped and what would be helpful to that other person? Would those be worthwhile conversations to have? What would you say? What would you do? What are the questions or concerns you would want to express?

5. Are you afraid of grief? What do you fear? What does it mean to you to be vulnerable? With whom, if anyone, can you be?

6. Do you have judgments about people in grief? They should take more time to grieve. They should be feeling better by now. What does that teach you about yourself? What do you want or need to do to be the person you want to be regarding asking for help and/or supporting other people who matter to you?

7. Grieving comes in all forms. Sometimes it is apparent that you or someone else is grieving. Sometimes not. Some people get super busy to avoid pain. Some people get angry. Some people get acquisitive. Some people talk more than usual or less than usual. If you wanted to help yourself or others, how would you sort out the clues to identify that you are grieving, that someone you care about is grieving? Then what?

8. What do you say to someone grieving so you don't make things worse? If you don't know, how do you figure it out?

9. If the grieving is around the loss of a healthy body, such as having cancer, the guidance is often given to just say, "I'll do this for you," rather than asking the person to let you know if you can do something or asking them what you can do. Those questions are often unanswerable to a person grieving or dealing with treatments. What might you say you can do?

10. Does grieving end, change, disappear, or can grief last forever? Does it return on anniversaries at other times of distress? That is, does grief end?

CATEGORY VII

CONTEMPLATING

Finding Your Voice

Triggers

Being Old. Being Young

Lightness and Darkness in Every Life

Softening Up or Toughening Up

Walking the Spiritual Path

Considering who you are and what your stories are that help you examine, notice, and imagine who you have been and who you are now, can bring you peace and comfort, wonder, disappointment, or distress. Pondering about your past can lead to reflection, evaluation, calm, clarity, learning, new ideas, and more. Pausing, being still, and increasing awareness can make an examined life more accessible. Even if what you notice is uncomfortable, movement is possible when you turn the light on whatever is there; it may be healing, helpful, redirecting, and while not always easy, certainly better.

FINDING YOUR VOICE

Finding your voice, being seen, or wearing a mask— as in hiding, speaking up, being quiet, waiting, pausing, or shutting down are ways to show up in your life, in your world, or not. Some people speak up most of the time, and some speak up infrequently, too little of the time, and do not say enough of what is important to them. If you are the talker or if you are the quiet one/listener, consider your motivation, your intention, your history, your models, your impact, your created or missed opportunities, your personal or impersonal way of being with others, the implications, and outcomes you want and those you get, intended or not.

Some people grew up being seen and cherished, loved for whom they were, and appreciated. Others were invisible, dismissed, discounted. Others felt and experienced being somewhere in between the two. Ask yourself whether the people who know you know the true you. Do you show your "good" side, the person you want to be, think you ought to be, imagine, is what is required of you to be if you are to be loved; is that who is showing up? Perhaps that is okay with you. Perhaps not. Perhaps there are parts of you that you value and others value too. Maybe there are parts of you that you wish would go away or you do not like. As you consider where you are at this point in your life, are you continuing what you experienced as a child, doing something other, and are you showing up as the person you want to be, wholly, partly, or at all?

Ask yourself each question offered. Consider responding to a question(s) that makes you smile, that you are attracted to answering, and to one or two you don't like or want to turn away from. Facing what you don't like, or are uncomfortable with, is often a path to the most significant learning. These questions are guides to prime or stimulate your memories and thoughts about your life. The questions are not intended to be answered in a literal manner. Read through each of them and react to the one(s) that open windows for you. Each life is unique, and the priming questions impact each of us differently.

SENSITIZING QUESTIONS AND PROMPTS

1. What does it mean to be seen? What does it mean to be invisible? Do you have an instance of one or both of those experiences in your early life, in your life now? What is better for you?

2. When you imagine what would give you a good and right life, what would you want to remain the same as is true now? What are two things that would change?

3. If someone knew you for a very long time, what would be their positive descriptors of you? How would you want them to describe you? If someone knew you for a very long time, what would be their less than positive description of you?

4. If someone near to you truly saw you, what would they discover that is not apparent to them now? Would, for example, they find out that you are much stronger than you let on? Or would they discover how tender and vulnerable you feel more often than you let on? Something else?

5. If you have been invisible, dismissed, or discounted, how do you continue to reinforce or encourage that happening? What do you do that increases the likelihood that you are not seen? Does that take care of you? What is one thing you might do to change that way of being if you so wished?

6. What does strutting your stuff mean to you? What does hiding or hesitating mean to you?

7. What does the outside world see when they see you? What do you want the world to see? Are they the same or different? If you took your mask off, what do you imagine/fear/long to have happen?

8. What does "finding your voice" mean?

9. Do you see yourself as someone who speaks up or someone who shuts down, waits, pauses, and asks others to talk first by asking questions? Is that okay? All the time? Some of the time? Never?

10. Who in your real life or who in an imagined life would you like to spend time with frequently? What do you find appealing on this continuum of speaking up or shutting down/being quiet/pausing/hesitating?

11. What are the good things about shutting down/listening/pausing/waiting/asking others to talk? What are the challenging things about that style? What is there to learn?

12. What are the good things about speaking up? What are the challenging things about that style? What is there to learn?

13. How would others describe you? If right now you asked five people who know you where they would see you on this continuum, what would they say? Would that be good, okay, not so good to you?

14. If you were to help a friend who does too much of one or the other things, where would you start? What would you say? How would you encourage that person to move in a direction that could make them more effective and feel better in their life? Does any of that apply to you?

15. When you consider how you got the way you are, now that you are considering this question, what missed opportunities have occurred because you do what you do? What experiences have you gained because you do what you do that you would not have had if you didn't do what you do?

16. Are there models you might keep inside of you who do what you think would be good? For example, if you need to speak up more, do you need an inner "Oprah" voice? If you need to shut down/be quiet/pause, do you need an inner "Obama" voice, someone who pauses and considers?

17. Can you imagine, can you let yourself imagine, that you said to someone what you actually, truly need and want to say? How would that be? What would encourage that? What would discourage you from doing that? So what? Can you imagine, can you let yourself imagine, that you didn't say to someone what you truly want to say because it is better not to do that? What would encourage that? What would discourage you from doing that? So what?

18. We do much of what we do or say automatically, instinctively, or intuitively, without thought or reflection. Now that the question is being raised, what values does this touch on for you? For example, can you complete the sentence, "A good or kind or thoughtful person. . .", "A bad or selfish or preoccupied person . . .", or some other value-laden belief?

19. On the personal vs. impersonal dimension, do you let in what others offer, whether you are the talker or even the listener, do you genuinely engage with others or not?

20. What does it mean to be seen? What does it mean to be invisible? Do you have an instance of one or both of those experiences in your early life, in your life now? What is better for you? How have those experiences impacted the choices you make in your life now?

TRIGGERS

We all have needs. We all want those needs met. This is normal. This is reasonable. The challenge comes when a need we have, legitimate or not, is not satisfied for whatever reason. Sometimes the cause is legitimate. Sometimes, not. Since every need we have at every minute will never be met, what matters is to notice, take stock, and see what happens when we get triggered; that is, we have a strong emotional reaction to our need that is not being met.

Triggers are different for different people. One person might be triggered — have a negative emotional response —to feeling "less than," and that would not even be something noticed by another person. Another person might be impacted by needing to be "right, " which would not matter to someone else. A third person might always want to be "nice" and feel horrible if they do something self-protective but are viewed negatively by someone else. Specific words can be triggering even though they are different for each of us. To someone, "divorce" will be hard to hear. For someone else, "old" will be hard to hear." Our triggers have a history. There are endless ways anyone can be triggered. What is essential is to identify, become aware of, and awake to what triggers you.

Usually, triggers are the result of what you needed as a child and did not get. If you never were listened to or felt seen as a child, you may have withdrawn to cope, or perhaps you were insistent and came forward, so you could not be denied. Either of those might be reactive responses rather than something that took care of you. Now, as an adult, it is necessary to see if what you do when you are triggered is helpful to you or not.

For example, when you are ignored or imagine you are being ignored, do you continue to shut down and withdraw as you did as a child? Or do you get more activated and become insistent on being heard and seen? Does the behavior you choose work for you? What other choices do you have? Would it be better now to be vulnerable and say, "I feel ignored?" "I need your attention." If anything, pause and consider what you want from a particular person. What else might take care of you?

If you are triggered by feeling left out, how can you help yourself? The goal here is to know what triggers you. Own it. Don't judge it. It was something you learned. Develop ways to manage yourself and see more choices for a better life.

Of course, while there is a wide range of triggering behaviors, there are also many responses. Becoming aware of your responses and reactions can give you more options of whether or not those responses and reactions are good and right for you. Many people get angry. Some withdraw and close off. Others go on the offensive. Sometimes people acquiesce with resentment or comply and please, charm. Maybe you blame others for their terrible behavior or shame them for doing what they did. Or, possibly, you eat, drink, shop, gamble, or just get busy, busy, busy, so you do not have to face your feelings.

Another choice. Notice the trigger(s). Notice your responses and reactions. Learn from them. See what else might take better care of you. Triggers will probably continue for a long time, maybe even forever. However, how you respond to your triggers can give you a better life. If you feel you are never triggered, look again!

Ask yourself each question offered. Consider responding to a question(s) that makes you smile, that you are attracted to answering, and to one or two you don't like or want to turn away from. Facing what you don't like, or are uncomfortable with, is often a path to the most significant learning. These questions are guides to prime or stimulate your memories and thoughts about your life. The questions are not intended to be answered in a literal manner. Read through each of them and react to the one(s) that open windows for you. Each life is unique, and the priming questions impact each of us differently.

SENSITIZING QUESTIONS AND PROMPTS

1. What are your triggers? Many people have written extensively and eloquently about triggers.

   There are endless examples. Almost anything can be triggering. A few frequently occurring ones—someone rejects you, leaves you, you feel helpless, discounted, ignored, blamed, or controlled, when you want or need to feel accepted, liked, appreciated, or respected.

2. Identify a few of your triggers. If you are not sure, think about what doesn't feel good to you. And, if you are not sure, ask the people around you; they will probably know what they are. Are triggers good and helpful? What is valuable about them? Are triggers bad and a problem? Why are they a problem? Do you trigger other people? How? Is that okay with you?

3. What do people you know, whether you like them or not, criticize you for doing or not? What is there to learn from what they are telling you? What do you do or not do, say or not say, when you are triggered?

4. What triggers do the people closest to you exhibit at work, home, school, dog park, or wherever? How does their behavior impact you, and what do they do?

5. What triggers did your parents demonstrate? Did you have judgments, positive or negative, about what you saw? Did you talk to them about what you saw? Did you complain? Did you stay quiet? What did you learn?

6. Do triggers get in your way of having relationships with people now? Who? How?

7. Where would you start if you need to be more expressive of your wants and needs? What would you say to whom? Will you?

8. Where would you start if you need to pull in and take care of your own needs and wants first rather than looking to other people? Will you?

9. If you were or are neglected in your life by the people around you, what do you do with those needs to be seen/heard/appreciated? How is that working for you?

10. Right now, make a list, if you wish, about what one or two triggers you want to tackle in your life? A way to start— what is the opposite of what you do now? If you talk too little, because your trigger is that you were ignored, what might you plan to do, today, to speak up with the next person you see? If you talk too much, because your trigger is that you were ignored, what might you plan to do today, to contain or get curious about the next person you see?

11. Everyone has stories about themselves, who we are, and how we are in this world. That story includes our triggers. We are both unconscious and conscious of them. Maybe you say, "I am a very nice person." You get triggered when someone does not appreciate your niceness. What do you do when you are not

appreciated? That may help you see your unconscious triggers. Or, maybe you say, "I am a very independent person." You get triggered when you find you need something from someone else; you don't like that. What do you do? That is probably unconscious triggered behavior.

12. Whom do you ignore? In your life, there are people with whom you interact and people you know but do not engage with fully. How come? What is there to learn from the selections you are making?

13. What is your first response when you are triggered? Your second response? Are they good, effective choices for you?

14. If you were to set an intention to try another way, what might that be? Would it make sense to you to notice that you are triggered and not do anything until you can feel more centered and see that what they are doing is about them and not about you (that is, not taking it personally)?

15. If your response to being triggered is to be busy, busy, busy, what feelings do you suppose you are avoiding? Is that okay with you? Maybe so? Maybe not?

16. Are there people in your life who trigger negative emotional responses and reactions you may want to talk to, and if they cannot be worked out, let go from your life?

17. Are there people in your life who trigger positive emotional responses and reactions with whom you may want to spend more time?

BEING OLD. BEING YOUNG

What does our age, that number, mean? When we turn into a new decade, a decade and a half, or when we have the nine at the end of the number—50, 55, 59—, our minds/thoughts/feelings are impacted. The consequence of that number is rooted in our history, experience, culture, individual health, and the context in which we live and with whom. Imagining ourselves as young or old, somewhere in between, as part of one labeled group or another, e.g., baby boomers, generation X, or the elderly, can have meaning, too. When you think of how you hold your place in the world vis a vis yourself at another time and those older or younger, you may feel enhanced or limited. How do you see yourself —young or old — and what is the impact?

Ask yourself each question offered. Consider responding to a question(s) that makes you smile, that you are attracted to answering, and to one or two you don't like or want to turn away from. Facing what you don't like, or are uncomfortable with, is often a path to the most significant learning. These questions are guides to prime or stimulate your memories and thoughts about your life. The questions are not intended to be answered in a literal manner. Read through each of them and react to the one(s) that open windows for you. Each life is unique, and the priming questions impact each of us differently.

SENSITIZING QUESTIONS AND PROMPTS

1. How old are you — actually? Physically? Emotionally? Health-wise? To your parent, alive or remembered? What other ways can you decide how old you are beside the number?

2. Does that age change or stay the same throughout the day, week, or year?

3. Is your age the same when you are with your family, friends, and coworkers? Is your age the same at work or at play?

4. What were your assumptions, and what were you taught about what it means to be your age? What is your perception of people who are younger or older than you, by a little or a lot?

5. Does age matter? Why? What does age mean? What does aging mean? What is the impact on you of the age of those around you?

6. Some medical people speak of aging like a car. You can take excellent care of it but, at some point, it becomes an old car. Do you relate to that idea?

7. What would you say to someone younger or older about aging?

8. What does it mean, to you, to celebrate a decade's birthday? Do you celebrate, sink into some feelings, try to ignore them, or something else? Do you have a plan? When the date of your birthday approaches, what do you recall of other birthdays?

9. If you could be the "perfect" age, what would it be? When was it, or when will it be?

10. Do you tell the truth if someone asks your age? Or not? How come? Why does talking about age even matter? Does it?

11. At what age are women or men their very best? Their very worst? What are you even talking about here?

12. What would you say to yourself exactly one year from today about what you want to feel about the coming year? Is this the best you will ever be, so maybe acknowledge that and enjoy it? Yes? No?

13. What would you say to yourself today about how young or old you are?

14. What do you most look forward to about getting older? What do you dread most about getting older?

15. What is the one-sentence guideline you have for yourself about aging? Is aging good or bad or neutral? Something in between?

LIGHTNESS AND DARKNESS IN EVERY LIFE

When we approach the concept of lightness and darkness, some immediate associations, thoughts, and feelings emerge. Lightness may be imagined, perceived, or seen as good and darkness as bad, evil, or difficult. As always, paying attention to lightness and darkness in our lives brings us to a more known place, increased self-awareness, and more available inner wisdom. Lightness can be good or other. Darkness can be good or other.

In the light, there may be energy, the ability to see more, both what we are happy to see and, possibly, what we would just as well not see. In lightness, there is the load that can be carried with ease. In lightness, life can be experienced as easier. Life may be experienced without looking at what one does not wish to look at. Light is easy. Light is good. Light is dancing, skipping. What is the other side? Light can be blinding, over-saturated, too much because all that is present may be observed. Darkness is depth, intensity, challenge, mystery, concern, and fright. Nighttime is often scarier. Yet, the morning light brings more illness. Darkness can be quiet, still, and peaceful. Lightness and darkness can mean time and place. Lightness and darkness can be a state of being. They can be exemplary and other. They can bring us questions and answers.

If you bravely look at what you see, what you turn toward, and what you have turned away from, there is the chance to know and be more of what you might be. There is consequence if you prefer or choose not to see lightness and darkness. Some people would say, so what, live life and do not seek or search. Others would say, I must always learn. Many people go on a quest for more of their inner life when they find they must do that to handle something that has emerged in life — loss, fear, worries, confusion, and other experiences. Whatever the catalyst, the choice of attending to lightness and darkness in your life sits waiting at your door. See if today is the day you open that door.

Ask yourself each question offered. Consider responding to a question(s) that makes you smile, that you are attracted to answering, and to one or two you don't like or want to turn away from. Facing what you don't like, or are uncomfortable with, is often a path to the most significant learning. These questions are guides to prime or stimulate your memories and thoughts about your life. The questions are not intended to be answered in a literal manner. Read through each of them and react to the one(s) that open windows for you. Each life is unique, and the priming questions impact each of us differently.

SENSITIZING QUESTIONS AND PROMPTS

1. What does light, lightness mean to you? What does dark, darkness mean to you? Are you drawn to or have an affinity for one or the other? How come?

2. Is that attraction, affinity to one side, one experience or the other, the way you have always been or something new?

3. In your current life, who represents lightness? Darkness? Who in your earlier life brought you lightness, darkness?

4. If you used to live in a dark place and now live in a light place or a more balanced place, what changed, and what moved you to where you are now? If you used to live in a light place and now live in a dark place or a less balanced place, what changed, and what moved you to where you are now?

5. Is it enlivening to focus on lightness in your life? Is lightness frothy, gentle, upbeat, elegant, or something else? Is lightness always good and positive? Does living with the lightness mean denying something dark that would be valuable to see? What is the downside of lightness?

6. If you are an optimist, some people would say genetically predisposed to see the light, good, positive, glass half full approach to life, how is that a better way to live? How is that a more problematic way to live your life?

7. If you are a pessimist, some people would say genetically predisposed or having learned to be this way as a result of the experiences you had, and you see the darkness, the disturbing, upsetting, troublesome, glass half empty way of living this life, how is that a better way to live? How is that a more problematic way to live your life?

8. Perhaps you are a fatalist, where everything is determined by fate, destiny, whatever is meant to happen will happen. Does that take you to the lightness or to the darkness?

9. "Someone I loved once gave me a box full of darkness. It took me years to understand that this too, was a gift." Mary Oliver. What does that mean to you?

10. Through the light of the silvery moon, you can find your way home. Or, in the darkness of the night, you may still find your way, just another way. What guides you?

11. As you begin each day, do you start in darkness? Or in lightness? What does that say to you about you?

12. Some people lead their lives with worry, anxiety, concern and see that as wisdom. Other people come from hope, wishes, and dreams. Is one good and the other not good? If you have mostly been one way, how would/could your life be so much better if you tried another way? Your instinctive self will always say, no way. If you bring more of your "choice-full" self to the question, what could make your life better, different, broader? What fears or doubts keep you doing something other than what you have always done?

13. Sometimes, we think we live in the light but only see what is within a few inches of our reality. If you back up, pause, reflect, what is the wildest vision and version of yourself you can imagine, conjure? You may think you have been living in the light; however, giving yourself more space to contemplate who you are and who you might be is another way to bring light into your life. What would that look like for you?

14. Darkness is so so good. Really? Yes. Time to pause. Time to wonder. Time to stop. Time for what for you?

15. Are fears a dark place? Are fears a chance for promise?

16. Who in your world lives in lightness? How do you know?

17. Who in your world lives in darkness? What does that look like to you?

18. If you live in darkness, what step might you take to see the other reality? If you live in lightness, what is a step to see a different reality, the opposite? Why would you take such a step? Why not?

19. Often, we do not know what we do not know about ourselves and the world. If you reflect on one or two things you have said or done in the recent past (month or two) that had you feel radiant, glowing, or exquisite, what would that have been? Did you notice at the time? If so, how was that? If not, how is that now? If, on the other hand, you recall one or two things you have said or done in the recent past (month or two) that had you feeling pensive, pained, or stopped, what time would that have been? Did you notice at the time? If so, how was that? If not, how is that now? Was one of these times good and the other not so good? Which was which? How come?

20. Is light less valued and dark more meaningful in your value system? Has more depth?

21. What message would you teach someone younger about how to bring lightness or darkness into their life?

22. If today is the last day of your reflection and you want to find the most meaningful and direct messages to yourself about what you want to bring into your life — the message of lightness, the message of darkness — what would those focal points be?

23. If someone was to honestly know you, capture your essence, and have a clear image of who you are, what is the one line that expresses that version of you?

24. If you are unafraid of life, what would you do and be different from what you are and do now?

25. Always looking at what matters in your life, considering the tension of the opposite sides of you, where is there to go from here?

SOFTENING UP OR TOUGHENING UP

Some people grew up having to be strong, tough, resilient, and independent. While their physical needs were met, their emotional needs were criticized, ignored, or dismissed. They grew up either looking for someone to give them what they didn't get or not expecting they would ever get what they needed. Hence, they became independent or even too independent, that is, not available for the relationships they want.

Waking up is a continuing process. No one wakes up once and for all. There is no limit to wakefulness, just as there is no limit to aliveness. It is risky to be awake to life. It takes courage. Rise to the risk of life, face the challenge of life, of love. Are you awake, asleep, doing/thinking/feeling what keeps you comfortable, or allowing yourself space and time to do/be/feel something else? Being alive is a process, not an outcome. There may be places where you are already awake or know you would be better served by letting go. Notice what is a stretch in responding to this question, not only what you have considered before.

Ask yourself each question offered. Consider responding to a question(s) that makes you smile, that you are attracted to answering, and to one or two you don't like or want to turn away from. Facing what you don't like, or are uncomfortable with, is often a path to the most significant learning. These questions are guides to prime or stimulate your memories and thoughts about your life. The questions are not intended to be answered in a literal manner. Read through each of them and react to the one(s) that open windows for you. Each life is unique, and the priming questions impact each of us differently.

SENSITIZING QUESTIONS AND PROMPTS

1. In your understanding, what is softening or toughing up in relationships with other people? How are you with some people and different with others? Who and why?

2. Are you soft and accommodating or tough and not so available? How do you know that to be so? Do you see that in yourself, or is that the information or feedback you have received from others? How is it to think of yourself in that way?

3. What is good or not so good, in your estimation, of being softer or tougher, or more of what you are not so much now?

4. Are there changes needed in your life, from your perspective, from the messages from other important people in your life—a friend, partner, child, or therapist? What changes?

5. Are you motivated to make active choices to try other ways of being, or is a passive approach that happens without your paying attention to it, more your style and preference? Or possibly you are fine just the way you are. Where do you fall on the continuum?

6. Is this framework of value to you as you imagine what successful growth and psychological development could bring to your life? What can you imagine would be particularly helpful as you live your life if you made some new choice(s)? What would they be?

7. When you meet someone who is accommodating, perhaps soft and gentle, do you move toward or away from them? How come? When you meet someone strong and sure, perhaps even formidable, do you have an affinity for that person, or do you move away? What can you learn about yourself from that awareness?

8. Do you have judgments about others who are soft or tough? Do you have judgments about yourself for those parts of yourself? What are those judgments?

9. Life circumstances may call upon us to be more of one or the other of these ways of being. What might those ways be, and have you been able to be "choice-full" at those times in a good and right way? If not, what would you imagine could help you show up the way you want the next time?

10. Softening up could be gentler, more thoughtful, and kind to others. Toughening up could be feeling bold and robust. What are your descriptors for this pair of opposites, and how would your life be better if you could have both parts of you available as you figure out how you will move through a particular experience?

WALKING THE SPIRITUAL PATH

Many pages have been written about spirit, spirituality, and walking a spiritual path. For some, contemplating, imagining, discerning, and considering is a way of life. Angeles Arrien wrote the outstanding book, *The Four-Fold Way: Walking the Paths of the Warrior, Teacher, Healer, and Visionary*, and taught many of us about this part of life. In her book, *Finding the On-Ramp to Your Spiritual Path: A Roadmap to Joy and Rejuvenation*, Jan Phillips wrote,

"To be on a spiritual path means to live mindfully, paying attention to the signs along the road and being conscious of our body — the vehicle we are traveling in — and of the needs and safety of others on the journey. To be on a spiritual path means to look inward as often as outward, knowing that the externals of our lives are reflections of our thoughts and words, manifestations of that which we are imagining and energizing into being with the fuel of our passion. To be on a spiritual path means using the rearview mirror to ensure that the path behind us is clear of debris and that we do not obstruct another's journey with our clutter. It means making peace with our past, knowing our future contains it, and summoning the courage it takes to acknowledge, forgive, and release whatever we have clung to that impedes our movement."

If spirit and spirituality are part of your active life, here is a chance to bring your psychological self to the questions raised here. If spirit and spirituality have not been a part of your life or are passive in your world, these questions may stir in you something to be explored.

Ask yourself each question offered. Consider responding to a question(s) that makes you smile, that you are attracted to answering, and to one or two you don't like or want to turn away from. Facing what you don't like, or are uncomfortable with, is often a path to the most significant learning. These questions are guides to prime or stimulate your memories and thoughts about your life. The questions are not intended to be answered in a literal manner. Read through each of them and react to the one(s) that open windows for you. Each life is unique, and the priming questions impact each of us differently.

SENSITIZING QUESTIONS AND PROMPTS

1. What do spirit, and spirituality mean to you? Is it an active, passive part of your life, something you have ever considered essential or not?

2. Is spirituality or religion important, enforced, encouraged, or nonexistent in your family of origin? As you grow up, has spirituality or religion become more or less important? How so? Is that okay with you?

3. If you are on a healing path, self-searching, seeking, wondering even, would exploring spirit, spirituality, or religion in any form be a helpful and worthwhile primary or adjunctive path to explore?

4. If you have a substantial interest in this part of life, how did you come to that curiosity and value? Who helped you? Are you imagining that doing more exploration here could help you stretch now?

5. If you have no interest in this part of life, what do you know about those feelings and thoughts? Is this a time to reconsider, or are you content with that way of being?

6. Are there teachers who taught you things you might find helpful to bring back into your life? Are there teachers who taught you some things that it would be better to let go of because of whatever, e.g., they were hurtful, limiting, wrong?

7. Are there teachers you want or have wanted to seek out? Who are they? Is now the time?

8. What questions come to mind that you might care to explore and find answers to for yourself now?

9. Is this aspect of life just not for you? Do you know why or care to know why?

10. What comes next for you about spirit, spirituality, or religion, if anything?

CATEGORY VIII

DISCERNING

Big Life. Little Life

Independence. Dependence. Are You Invested In One and Need To Find The Other?

Permanence. Impermanence

Risks Taken. Risks Not Taken

Rules Of Your Life: The Latest and Greatest, The Old Standbys, What Is Right?

Truth and Fiction: What Is True In Your Life? What Is Fiction? What Is Clear? What Is Distorted?

Waking Up To … Letting Go Of …

Actively choosing, carefully distinguishing in your mind how you have lived your life, gives you a chance to review and differentiate what might be right and good for you as you move forward. Many think we consciously decide what we are doing now and in the future. More frequently, though, we instinctively, automatically do what we do, think what we think. These themes ask you to take a deeper look. At first, for example, you might say, I just have a few "rules" by which I live. What is almost always true is that we each have a zillion rules that guide us through each day. When you invite or allow yourself the chance to stop and look at those guiding rules in the light of day, many of them, maybe 95 percent of them, will still work for you. The discovery is in finding what does not fit for you now. Discerning calls for that reflection.

BIG LIFE. LITTLE LIFE

As time passes, many senses, memories, expectations, and feelings get stirred. Some of those are good, positive, hopeful, or energizing. Some may be challenging, sad, difficult, or enervating. For some people having a grand experience with relevant people is a requirement. For others, a few quiet moments of reflecting and imagining make the time right. As you consider and take stock about whether a big life or little life is your desire, what would that mean for you? Big and little can be events, thoughts, things, ideas, creations, imaginings, or something else entirely. Choosing may be what is most important. Not choosing is choosing, too.

Ask yourself each question offered. Consider responding to a question(s) that makes you smile, that you are attracted to answering, and to one or two you don't like or want to turn away from. Facing what you don't like, or are uncomfortable with, is often a path to the most significant learning. These questions are guides to prime or stimulate your memories and thoughts about your life. The questions are not intended to be answered in a literal manner. Read through each of them and react to the one(s) that open windows for you. Each life is unique, and the priming questions impact each of us differently.

SENSITIZING QUESTIONS AND PROMPTS

1. What is big for you? What is little for you? What is your first instinct about how you would best experience this next season of your life?

2. If you let your imagination condense and identify the smallest elements that will make life just how you want it to be in the season, what must be included? Excluded? What would be included if you let your imagination expand to its greatest size, with the grandness of every sort? Excluded?

3. Big or little may not be how you usually define or assess what occurs in your life or how you plan your life. What would be different if you used these parameters? For example, if you always think about small, incremental ways to change your life, what might happen if you considered the large change/addition/variation in how and what you do? Or, if you always think big, what will happen if you focus on the tiny elements that might, this next month and beyond, touch you deeply and fully, even if just for one moment?

4. Is this season about big or little things, numbers of people, newness/oldness, goodness/badness, the familiar/unfamiliar? What if you did the opposite this year? What could happen?

5. If you are someone who takes more than you give, what would be the big or little change that would alter you, your way of being? Or, if you give more than you take, what would be the big or little change that would alter you, your way of being?

6. Is "big" for children and "little" for adults?

7. Is "big" selfish and "little" selfless?

8. Is "big" bad and "little" good?

9. Do you live a big life or small life? If you considered the opposite, what would be different today, or tomorrow?

10. Who among those you know encourages your "bigness" or your "smallness"?

11. Who do you know and admire who is "big" in whatever ways? Who do you know and admire who is "little" in whatever ways? Do you have something to learn from that person? What would it be?

12. Is big a state of mind or a way of being? Is little a state of mind or a way of being?

13. Focusing only on you, what is one step that moves you away from where you have always been — big or little – towards a new you?

INDEPENDENCE. DEPENDENCE. ARE YOU INVESTED IN ONE AND NEED TO FIND THE OTHER?

Being independent and being dependent are each positive. At specific times of life, with particular people, certain circumstances, or as an ongoing way of being, the place one is on this continuum will determine what one says or does, doesn't say, or doesn't do. Some of us revel in being independence, and the idea of dependence on anyone else is unappealing. Others want to be watched over by others and look for or seek out people to care for them. If you are invested in one end of the continuum, you probably can barely imagine the value of the opposite side.

As with any aspect/trait/voice, both sides are good, valuable, and necessary to have in the mix as we choose what will be best for us. Being free of influence, control, and reliance on others can be desirable. And it can have self-limiting consequences. Being dependent can mean accepting support, ideas, and reciprocity. Dependence on others can be desirable, and it can have self-limiting effects. As you recall the choices you have made in your life, most people have a clear and distinct predisposition to one end of this continuum or the other. As with other traits, there may be an associated judgment of people on the opposite end. Notice where you have been. Imagine what the value could be if you made choices from the opposite perspective.

Really. Imagine whether surrendering can be a strength or not. Imagine whether taking charge can be a strength or not. A particular challenge with this pair of opposite parts of ourselves is that we may think we are independent, but we are quite dependent on others for our self-esteem, stability, finances, or something else. We may think we are dependent, but we do take charge of things and fail to recognize that trait within us because it would or might cause discomfort. This pair of opposites and how they influence your functioning can be surprising.

Ask yourself each question offered. Consider responding to a question(s) that makes you smile, that you are attracted to answering, and to one or two you don't like or want to turn away from. Facing what you don't like, or are uncomfortable with, is often a path to the most significant learning. These questions are guides to prime or stimulate your memories and thoughts about your life. The questions are not intended to be answered in a literal manner. Read through each of them and react to the one(s) that open windows for you. Each life is unique, and the priming questions impact each of us differently.

SENSITIZING QUESTIONS AND PROMPTS

1. When you first hear the words "being independent" and "being dependent," what is your response? What about mutual dependence or interdependence? Are they more okay or less okay? If you have ever thought about the question of independence and dependence, have you just known that "the good and right way for you to be is . . .?"

2. What is independence? What is dependence? How do you define them? What judgments do you bring to each of them? Take time, if you choose, to look at the positive and negative judgments you make about being independent and being dependent. Write them down. Who taught you those ideas? Were those judgments helpful to you at one point in your life? Are they still useful? Are they impeding you in some way? How?

3. Who in your life, current or past, would you see as "independent" or "dependent?" Did you or do you have an opinion about that person and how they were? Is it the same now as it was then? How has it changed if it has? What might you learn from that person's choices?

4. Sometimes, one is forced to become independent because their life situation changes suddenly and dramatically, not by their own choice. Sometimes, one is forced to become dependent because their life situation changes suddenly and dramatically, not by their own choice. Which would be harder for you? If you think about that circumstance (going in either direction), what might you think, do, or consider mitigating or lessen the impact, if possible?

5. Can you explain why the way of being opposite to where you are now is better? For example, if you are invested in being independent, what do you miss out on being or doing because you will not let others in your life provide something more? What do you get by being independent — safety that you won't be let down or something else? If you are invested in being dependent on others, look carefully here because often, the person who believes they are fiercely independent is highly dependent on another person for support, stability, love, connection, money, status, or something else. What do you get by being dependent? How does it give you good things? How does it limit you?

6. Are you both independent and dependent? When, where, with whom? As you look at this in the light of day, now what? Is that working for you?

7. What are five positive characteristics of being dependent? What are five negative attributes of being dependent? What are five positive aspects of being independent? What are five negative attributes of being independent?

8. To whom are you attracted, on the independent and dependent scale, in friendships, partners, and other important people in your life? To whom are you repelled?

9. If you want to explore the opposite end of the spectrum, what would be your biggest challenge? What would be your biggest hoped-for reward?

10. Where would you start if you were to help your "good friend" move along this continuum? What would you say to them to help motivate them to make a change or two? How would you support them?

11. Independence and dependence, as themes in your life, can relate to the many varied aspects of one's life. You could be independent or dependent regarding mobility, finances, opportunities to experience certain things, etc. What would be easiest for you? What would be hardest? What does that mean to you?

12. What could you do if you imagine trying out the opposite way of being? For example, if you are independent, and pride yourself on that, try out, in your mind or writing, what it would look like if you became dependent for a day. Who and what would you seek? What would you have wished you had

done before that experiment to be more fully ready for it? If you are dependent and pride yourself on that, try out, in your mind or writing, what it would look like if you became independent for a day. What would be different? How would your life change? Take stock.

13. Dependence and independence are traits that may differ in different circumstances. Maybe it is okay to be independent where your work is concerned, but in your personal relationships, you want mutual dependence, interdependence, or something else. Maybe, it is okay to depend on a partner but not your children, friends, or family. Where, when, and with whom is it okay to be dependent or independent?

14. If it is a year from now and you had made one, two, or three changes to becoming more of what you have less of now, how would your life be different? Would that be good?

15. Whose help would you seek to make those changes?

16. Now what?

PERMANENCE. IMPERMANENCE

Many have written about permanence and impermanence, studied, explored, and considered it. Look at what comes up for you when you consider what you hold, wish, want, need to be, feel, and experience permanent; make this concept personal, meaningful, and valuable. Is anything permanent? Is something permanent if it exists today? Is a relationship with a child, a partner, a friend, or an idea, fixed or constantly evolving? Does it matter?

You can explore these ideas as a concept. Or you can consider thinking about it regarding something personal. What is here for you? If something exists tomorrow, is it permanent or impermanent? Is everything impermanent? How do you live your life today, knowing that things may be different tomorrow?

We study, read about, and perhaps know the wisdom that permanence is an illusion. Everything is impermanent; within that awareness, we live our lives. That can and may inform how and what we do, the paths we take, the ideas we hold dear, and the opportunities taken or not. Against this backdrop, knowing of impermanence, the question becomes how can and does that enhance, enrich, enliven, embolden, and expand your life? Where does it limit your life? In the same way, we know that death is part of living, and if we live with that awareness of death each day, we may do and make different selections about where to place our energy.

This is the quest for what is worthy, in the tiniest sense and the most significant meaning of the question. As you consider where to focus, right now, for ten whole seconds, and notice if there is something different after those ten seconds have passed. Is there a pleasure here or there? Is there an ache here or there? Is there a thought, an idea, a wonder here or there? Is there a color here or there that was not in your consciousness ten seconds before? Now, what is worthy to you this day, week, or month? How do you know? Are there some criteria? Are there some areas that are forbidden?

Permanence and impermanence. They are. They are significant. They are real.

Ask yourself each question offered. Consider responding to a question(s) that makes you smile, that you are attracted to answering, and to one or two you don't like or want to turn away from. Facing what you don't like, or are uncomfortable with, is often a path to the most significant learning. These questions are guides to prime or stimulate your memories and thoughts about your life. The questions are not intended to be answered in a literal manner. Read through each of them and react to the one(s) that open windows for you. Each life is unique, and the priming questions impact each of us differently.

SENSITIZING QUESTIONS AND PROMPTS

1. What is permanence? What is impermanence? What do you wish, need, or want to be permanent? What is impermanent? If something is impermanent, does it still matter? How do you cope with the idea that nothing is forever? What is the implication of that idea? If you imagine, consider, write, or ponder the question of permanence and impermanence in your life, what is the consequence of that awareness? What does the question give you? Does it enhance your life? Does it complicate your life?

2. If something or some things are happening that you are just thrilled to be experiencing, do you want it or them to go on forever?

3. If something is happening that you want to end, does knowing it will end comfort you?

4. Knowing everything has a beginning and end can be a good thing, a bad thing, or something else. Of course, it matters what that thing is. Or does it?

5. What is the tiniest thing or two, the very smallest you can imagine, something minor, that if it went away would be good, if you remembered it was impermanent and would be gone?

6. What is an enormous thing or two, the largest you can imagine, that if it went away would be good, if you remembered it was impermanent and would be gone?

7. What are the most permanent things in life? Death and taxes are what usually come up. Beyond that, what is permanent in life? Why does it matter?

8. If today were all you knew existed, what are three things you would do right now that are good choices? Are you ready to do them? Are you stopping right this minute and doing one or two or three of them before you read another word?

9. Who in your world would understand your talking to them about what you are writing about, thinking about here as you consider these questions? Is there someone or more than one person? What would you want to say to them to invite a conversation about permanence and impermanence? Is that okay if there is no one with whom you would like to have such a discussion? If not, what can you do, will you do, and when?

10. Life can be challenging and is, for everyone, at least sometimes. M. Scott Peck, in his book, *The Road Less Traveled*, begins by saying, "Life is difficult." What is the truth of this idea, the impact, the implication for you?

11. What is worthy of you? Who is worthy of you? What are you doing, giving your time and attention to that, on reflection, is satisfying, good, positive, and right for you? Who are you living your life with, who, on review, is worth it? What and who are you involved with? Are your time and life well spent? If not, what then?

12. Is there greater comfort in the idea of permanence or impermanence?

13. Tabula rasa is the concept of a clean slate. Babies are thought to come into this world with a new beginning, where everything is fresh and to be determined. If you took a day, an hour, a moment, and made it something new, fresh, unexpected for you, imagining that the next moment, hour, or day, could bring a return to what you knew before, what freshness would you bring into your life today? Today! If everything is impermanent, perhaps you could let yourself imagine far out of your box of what is okay for you. How big or small can you let yourself imagine something new, unexpected, taboo, forbidden, unexplored, denied, not ever considered for you? Can you allow yourself to make a list of what would be excellent for you, remembering everything is impermanent? What is on that list?

14. Many of us have the great fortune to live the lives we do. Is that your sense of your life? If so, what do you appreciate? If not, what do you need, want?

15. Sometimes what we do becomes a type of permanence because we keep doing it. If what we do is good, terrific, keep doing what we do. Often, though, we keep doing things that would be better to stop doing or alter. Since it is often hard to know what would be better not to do or not do the same way, there is a challenge here. What, though, can you recall that you do or don't do that ends up with you feeling great? What can you remember that you do or don't do that ends up with you feeling bad or somewhere between tolerable and bad? Can you let yourself make a list? Then what? Can you tackle one item on that list?

16. Celebrations. Does the wonder and goodness in your life get fully appreciated remembering that you may never revisit it? Can you ever let yourself shout from the rooftop, "Look at me! I am fabulous! I am worthwhile! I am good!" If so, when did that happen? If not, when will it? If not, how come? Who will be there to cheer and clap? What would you invite? Who would be thrilled for you? Who would say, "You rock!" Who would think negatively about your doing that vs. thinking you are so cool about doing this? Hmmm. What about the nay-sayers in your life?

17. If this life is over tomorrow, have you done what counts and been with whoever counts today? If so, breathe deeply and notice. If not, what do you do tomorrow?

RISKS TAKEN. RISKS NOT TAKEN

Some people like safety. Others prefer risk-taking. Even so, with a preferred disposition, many of us do some of each. Risk may be taking a chance, such as not knowing or being unsure of the outcome, even approaching danger, doing something out of one's comfort zone, or the unfamiliar, it may also mean doing something other than what we were taught, what like-minded people would do, what people in our socioeconomic group, do or don't do. Risks can be great or small. They can be impactful or fleeting. They can have known or unknown consequences.

We often take risks and do not even know we are taking a risk. While we know that driving a car is a risk, it is not something most of us struggle to decide if we will do or not do. While we understand that getting into a relationship is a risk, most of us don't think of that as risk-taking. There is a risk in getting close to someone. A worthwhile risk. A necessary risk. Just not something we usually or primarily think of as a risk.

Taking a risk or not taking a risk may be the same thing. Perhaps everything is a risk. If you take it, you have one set of consequences. If you do not take it, you are not home free because there is always the lost opportunity, the missed experience, the what if? Each of us has taken risks, doing something when we could not know for sure the outcome, even if we thought we did. Then there is chance. The unknown. The unexpected. In some areas of our lives, we may be more or less willing, more or less likely, to take a risk. In other areas, we go for it. At the end of the day, what we do or don't do shows us who we are. The question to consider is how is that working for me?

Ask yourself each question offered. Consider responding to a question(s) that makes you smile, that you are attracted to answering, and to one or two you don't like or want to turn away from. Facing what you don't like, or are uncomfortable with, is often a path to the most significant learning. These questions are guides to prime or stimulate your memories and thoughts about your life. The questions are not intended to be answered in a literal manner. Read through each of them and react to the one(s) that open windows for you. Each life is unique, and the priming questions impact each of us differently.

SENSITIZING QUESTIONS AND PROMPTS

1. What risks have you taken in your life? As you reflect on those risks, what do you notice? What do you feel? What do you learn from those risks taken? What risks did you not take? What do you notice as you reflect on those times you did not take the risk? What do you feel? What can you learn from those risks you chose not to take? If you had to do it over, would you do the same thing? Something different? The opposite? Something incremental?

2. At this time of your life, are you in a position where you are considering, deciding about taking a risk or not taking that risk? What is the risk? What will you do? How will you choose? What help do you need to decide? Are you waiting? Are you frozen? Are you in the process of moving in one direction or another? Do you need help? From whom? Do you imagine the answer will just come to you? Is there something more active to do?

3. In our lives, frequently, there is the choice to take a risk or not. What significant risks in your life are you choosing to avoid or ignore? How come? What would happen if you turned toward those risks?

What is your fear? How can you manage or mitigate your anxiety to look at the risk waiting for your attention? What will happen if you continue to look away? The question to consider — if you knew you couldn't fail, what risk would you take?

4. Are you a risk taker? Do you avoid risk? How do you know that is an accurate description of yourself? Are you surprised, or is that how you have thought about yourself throughout your life?

5. Were you more of a risk taker at an earlier age? Did you take fewer risks when you were younger? What happened to change you?

6. Who do you know, now or in the past, whom you would label as a risk taker, a risk avoider? Did you have positive or negative judgment about that person and what they did, or why they did it if you knew? If you had questions to ask of that person (or people), what would you want to know?

7. Do you have experience, from close up or as an observer, of someone who took big risks and someone who chose not to?

8. Were your parents risk-takers or not? Did you wish they were more of the other than how they were? For example, they never moved from the home where you grew up, and you imagined they might have had a better life if they had tried something or somewhere new? Or they moved from house to house, and you wished they would have settled down somewhere, created roots, and had a long-time, stable home?

9. What would you consider a significant risk for you today?

10. What is the most significant risk you have ever taken? What is the biggest risk you chose not to take? What do you think about those decisions now?

11. What have you learned from a risk taken or not taken? How is your life different as a result of which option you took?

12. Do you believe life is all about chance? You can choose, plan, research, and consider, but the outcome will be what it will be at the end of the day.

13. Do you believe you can and do direct much of your life? If so, how have you done?

14. When you grow up, do you want to be a risk taker? Do you want to be more cautious and careful when you grow up? If you are grown up, what do you notice?

15. Do you think/believe that taking a risk or not taking a risk is the same thing? If you do one thing you are not doing something else.

16. If someone invites you into a risky situation or asks if you would consider a risky behavior — the risk can be emotional, physical, financial, or other things, too — what is your first response? What is second? What is third? Then what?

17. Are some kinds of risks easier and others harder for you? Are emotional risks easier or harder for you? Are physical risks easier or harder for you? Are financial risks easier or harder for you? What other kinds of risks do you encounter in your life?

18. What risks taken are you most proud of having taken? What risks not taken were so right that you can now breathe a sigh of relief that you didn't do what you could have done?

19. What risks taken are you embarrassed about, have shame about, wish you had never done, even if you learned something from them? What risks not taken are you embarrassed about, disappointed you didn't do or feel remorse about not doing?

20. What risks do you want to take now or within the next few years of your life? What are the steps to make those wishes a reality?

21. To people who care about you and want to know you better, what story or stories would you want them to hear about you as someone who has taken risks?

22. Have your risky choices been a way to conform to what others, your partner, caregivers, parents, and friends wanted you to do, influenced you to do? Have the risks not taken been influenced or affected by those people?

23. Do you worry about looking "good," "cool," "hip," and "in the know" so you take risks to look a certain way to certain people?

24. For you, is risk-taking or risks not taken a way to fit in? For example, you drink to fit in with the people who drink even though you know that is risky behavior for you.

25. Do you and your family of origin see risk similarly? If not, what is the difference?

26. Do you and your close friends or partners see risk similarly? If not, how does that work? Do you feel stifled? Do you feel discomfort? Do you appreciate the differences as a way to find your grounding? Something else? How do you bridge the gap if you live with someone who is risk-averse and you like risks? If you are more risk averse and live with someone who believes the universe will provide, everything will work out; how do you bridge that gap? What do you do if you cannot bridge that difference? How important and difficult is it for you to see things in very different ways?

27. If some other potentially meaningful relationship includes this difference in risk tolerance, how close to that person can you be?

28. Risk management is sometimes defined as the identification, analysis, assessment, control, and avoidance, minimization, or elimination of unacceptable risks. Sometimes the concept is the cost-benefit ratio or the risk-benefit ratio. Is this concept useful to you as you review your risk-taking dilemmas? Do you want to push yourself in one direction or another? How do you manage the movement from your comfort zone to another way of being?

29. Sometimes, life is our teacher. A risk taker becomes more cautious. A risk avoider takes more risks. Usually, something precipitates that movement. If this has happened to you, what was it, and are you good with the change? If not, do you need to find someplace in the middle or change back?

30. One way you become more aware of your risks taken/not taken choices is to look very carefully at how you define yourself and see yourself. Most people who do self-exploration think of themselves as having certain attributes. That is, you may think of yourself as someone responsive to others. If you took the risk of seeing yourself as being self-serving, that is, being sure, sure, to take care of your own needs first, would that present some risks for you? How would that be if you were certain to take exquisite care of yourself in your life? If that is a risk, what is the risk? How can you manage that risk? How can you take a step on that path? What happens if you look away? What happens if you deny that option?

RULES OF YOUR LIFE: THE LATEST AND GREATEST, THE OLD STANDBYS, WHAT IS RIGHT?

Our lives are defined by the choices we make. Those choices come from our personal history and collective history, which are culture-bound and time-bound. Some people follow the rules they learned. Some people do not. Some people follow their personally created rules. Some people live by them in an exact way and find that to be what is right for them. Some people loosely follow the rules. Some people do neither but have their own idea of what is right. Each way can be positive or not. What are the rules for your life?

Ask yourself each question offered. Consider responding to a question(s) that makes you smile, that you are attracted to answering, and to one or two you don't like or want to turn away from. Facing what you don't like, or are uncomfortable with, is often a path to the most significant learning. These questions are guides to prime or stimulate your memories and thoughts about your life. The questions are not intended to be answered in a literal manner. Read through each of them and react to the one(s) that open windows for you. Each life is unique, and the priming questions impact each of us differently.

SENSITIZING QUESTIONS AND PROMPTS

1. What is a rule? How do you define "rule"? Are rules mandates, guidelines, or suggestions? What is your attitude toward the idea of rules?

2. Where did your rules come from, and from whom? Can you adapt the rules you have learned or been taught?

3. Are some rules more important, primary, basic, or essential?

4. Famous sayings from your family sometime imply, connote, or communicate rules. What were the regular "messages" or "rules" you grew up hearing or were suggested and required directly and indirectly?

5. What are your rules for yourself? What are your rules for others? Are they the same? Are they different? What do you notice?

6. When do rules help, and when do they get in the way?

7. What rules do you have for personal relationships? Professional relationships?

8. What are your rules for living, regarding . . . time, work, health, relationships, money, values, hopes, dreams, wishes, birthdays/special occasions, holidays, children, or whatever?

9. How did you learn or create the rules for your life? Did you seem destined to follow them or did you stumble into them seemingly by chance? Did other people urge you to pursue these rules, or did they just seem to come to you? Did any childhood interests or experiences influence or direct your path?

10. When did you develop the rules for your life? How much choice do you have? How much choice did you feel you had?

11. What do you experience when you follow a primary rule in your life? When you don't?

12. Whom do you know who "broke" the rules in ways you admire?

13. Are some rules meaningful and helpful at one time but do not serve you now? What are they? Is there a new rule you want to try out?

14. Are you a benevolent rule maker or a strident one? Something else?

15. If you suspended all or some of your rules for even one day, what would happen? One hour? Would that be worth exploring? Or not?

16. Are you willing to negotiate your rules with a partner, friend, child, family member, or coworker?

17. What would your partner or best friend say about how your life reflects your rules?

18. What do you do when you have competing rules or expectations with someone with whom you are trying to form, develop, or maintain a relationship?

19. As you sit with yourself today, are there rules you think, want, or need to let go of, now, once and for all?

20. What are three positive guiding rules in your current life? What rule(s) would give you a better life? What rules interfere with your having the life you want?

21. How do rules help guide and organize your life?

22. If there was a global rule that you think everyone should have, what would it be?

TRUTH AND FICTION: WHAT IS TRUE IN YOUR LIFE? WHAT IS FICTION? WHAT IS CLEAR? WHAT IS DISTORTED?

Some people tell the truth about who they are to themselves and others. Some people think they are telling the truth but are creating fiction for many different reasons. Some people see themselves clearly, and others distort their reality. Both may be necessary to live, survive and thrive. What is your reality now? The real, the ideal, and the social self *make up our narrative self, or the self we tell ourselves we are.* The social self refers to how we think other people view us; the real self is the self we tell ourselves we are, and the ideal self is the self we would like to be. Some people tell themselves the truth, while others make things up knowingly and often for perceived good reasons. Some people distort, ignore, enhance, forget, and more as they move through their lives.

Take time to consider both sides: where, when, and with whom are you the most honest, accurate, realistic, and where, when, and with whom do you shade, change, or distort what is actual and true. Let yourself wonder why. The truth may be in the details. What is true about you? What is fiction? What is clear? What is distorted?

Ask yourself each question offered. Consider responding to a question(s) that makes you smile, that you are attracted to answering, and to one or two you don't like or want to turn away from. Facing what you don't like, or are uncomfortable with, is often a path to the most significant learning. These questions are guides to prime or stimulate your memories and thoughts about your life. The questions are not intended to be answered in a literal manner. Read through each of them and react to the one(s) that open windows for you. Each life is unique, and the priming questions impact each of us differently.

SENSITIZING QUESTIONS AND PROMPTS

1. What is your initial view of how you are in the world? In your inner life? With certain others? Who? Honest? Enhanced? Diminished? Are you truthful? Do you ignore, distort, or avoid? Are you clear, fuzzy, or somewhere in between? How is that?

2. What change(s)do you want to make now, if any, to align your truth saying or fiction saying in your life? For example, would it serve you better to be less truthful in certain situations and with particular people? Or would it be more enjoyable to create some stories or fiction or fantasy about yourself that might lead you in new, unexpected directions? Or would it be better for you to be brutally honest with yourself about some aspect of a person or people in your life? Or does distortion allow you to do things and be places you need or want to be, even though they are not perfect? If you allow yourself to be fuzzy about some situation, does that save you pain, or give you pain? Or do you keep yourself so busy that you get not even consider this question? Or?

3. Why might you be telling yourself and the world about yourself in the way you do? Is there a better way, a way that is more in line with whom you want to be?

4. Are you a "truth say-er" about who you are? Do you tell yourself good and bad things about yourself, or do you ignore some essential aspect(s) of who you are? Something else? How do your self-perceptions match the responses you get from people around you?

5. Are you a "truth say-er" about the significant people around you? Do you let yourself see the good and bad things about them, their strengths, and weaknesses, or do you distort and only see what you want to see?

6. Do the people around you support your view, or do they challenge your perception of you? Do you listen? Do you consider what they say even if you are not comfortable? Do you ignore them? How come? What might happen if you considered what another person sees in you might be helpful for you to see?

7. What about your perceptions and truths help you move forward in your life? What about your perceptions and truths keeps you stuck, limited, or even in trouble?

8. If you tend to see the rosy side of everything, what is the opposite? What is the opposite if you tend to see the dark side of everything? How would it serve you to be sure to check the other side of your reality? How would it limit you to be looking at both sides?

9. Is truth always good and fiction always bad? Is fiction always good and truth always bad? When is one better than the other?

10. What happens to you when you encounter someone who says their truth, and it is something that is very much what you see and experience with them? What happens to you when you meet someone who speaks their truth and what you experience is very different?

11. If you were to celebrate one truth about you that has meaning for you, what would that truth be, and how might you celebrate it? If you were to challenge one truth about you that you have concerns about, what would that truth be, and how might you challenge yourself to address those concerns?

12. What would be on that list if you make a list of what is true for you about the other important people in your life? What would be on that list?

13. If you list your distortions, partial-truths, and fiction in your life, what would they be?

14. If you pay attention to the people you have an affinity with what is it about them that draws you to them? Are they truthful, direct, straightforward, as best you can know? Or are they storytellers, enhancers, people who embellish and distort? Since both can be positive, what is it about that pull that helps you see something more about yourself?

15. What are three positive and three negative aspects of distortions or fiction? What are three positive and negative aspects of truth saying? Perhaps, if you consider this question, it behooves you to write about distortions, fiction, and truth.

WAKING UP TO . . . LETTING GO OF . . .

Waking up is a continuing process. No one wakes up once and for all time. There is no limit to wakefulness, just as there is no limit to aliveness. It is risky to be awake to life. It takes courage. Rise to the risk of life, face the challenge of life and love. Are you awake, asleep, doing or thinking, or feeling what keeps you comfortable or allowing yourself space and time to do or be or feel something else? Being alive is a process, not an outcome. There may be places where you are already awake or know you would be better served by letting go. Notice this question's stretch, not only what you have considered at another time in your life.

Ask yourself each question offered. Consider responding to a question(s) that makes you smile, that you are attracted to answering, and to one or two you don't like or want to turn away from. Facing what you don't like, or are uncomfortable with, is often a path to the most significant learning. These questions are guides to prime or stimulate your memories and thoughts about your life. The questions are not intended to be answered in a literal manner. Read through each of them and react to the one(s) that open windows for you. Each life is unique, and the priming questions impact each of us differently.

SENSITIZING QUESTIONS AND PROMPTS

1. What does being awake mean? How do you know you are?

2. Letting go of what you want to let go of can be meaningful. When you allow yourself to think the unthinkable, or what is just uncomfortable, what do you learn about yourself?

3. If you "listen" to what you have been told by people who love you, rather than people who tell you they love you, what would they ask you to wake up to knowing or seeing or feeling, and what would they ask you to let go of, now?

4. What is the most significant stretch for you to make today?

5. What is the most significant stretch for you to make that would require or demand another person in your life to do something different than is true today?

6. If you are going to consider letting go of …(whatever), what is on your list to consider? How would you order that list from the most important to you to the least important? What are the criteria? What would be the easiest to the hardest?

7. What makes a good day? What would make a good day better?

8. How can you remember, each day, what it means to be alive?

9. What do you do that takes you away from being in the present? For example, do you check your cell phone at dinner with a friend?

10. If you were going to ask someone with whom you spend time to remind you that you are drifting away from them, what would you ask them to say or do?

11. What does it mean to take a vacation from being awake and live? When is that okay with you?

12. What do you wish you would do, say, or feel today to move to aliveness?

13. What do you wish you would avoid doing to keep you out of touch with your preferences?

14. In three months, if you had done what you decided to do to choose life rather than drifting, how would you feel, and in what way would your life be different from today?

15. If you had let go of something (s) that are getting in the way of having the life you want, in what specific way would your life be better, and would you be more alive?

CATEGORY IX

CELEBRATING

Firsts. Lasts. Holidays and Other Occasions

Happy Birthday: The Real, The Remembered, The Hoped For

Uncovering Treasures That Matter: A Thing. A Person. An Experience

Commemorating who, what and the experiences that are extra special to you are the stories to consider here. It is time to attend to and pay attention to the meaning and significance of those times in your life that are milestones. Some, of course, are more important than others. Pause. Reflect. Consider what is celebratory and worth giving extra energy, time, and investment to. Celebrations are frequently complex experiences, especially because we bring expectations, hopes, wishes, and beliefs to them. Thinking about celebrating has some of us turn away and not want to be the center of things. Others want the roaring crowd. How to manage those differences is often part of the stories, that is, what worked, what didn't, and should there be a redo?

FIRSTS. LASTS. HOLIDAYS AND OTHER OCCASIONS

We usually know when we do something for the first time and rarely know it is the last time. What are the "first" and "last" elements of a holiday season or other significant times for you? Sometimes, by choice, we decide that we should add a "first" and make sure this is a "last." Consider what might be on your lists and how to make that happen.

In being awake for one's life and not assuming it will just go on forever, making active choices is the route to having the life you want and might mean no regrets. Many people want things to be upbeat or happy, or all good. When the reality is not that, they turn away from what is happening. Many people experience life as challenging and filled with longing. As the holidays or other significant occasions approach consider the possibility that what happens this year can have its firsts and lasts— with its configuration of people, place, and possibilities— how can you make this season be what truly takes care of you and the significant people in your life? If you bring into your consciousness the possibility that next year will be different from now, can you create or compose or allow it to be what will be good and right so that whatever happens next is as it must be? Take time to ponder, allow, and imagine, with your head, heart, and soul, what would make the next holiday season or special occasion be what you need it to be—face head on what gets in your way, if anything. See what will make whatever is first and whatever is last what you need it to be.

Ask yourself each question offered. Consider responding to a question(s) that makes you smile, that you are attracted to answering, and to one or two you don't like or want to turn away from. Facing what you don't like, or are uncomfortable with, is often a path to the most significant learning. These questions are guides to prime or stimulate your memories and thoughts about your life. The questions are not intended to be answered in a literal manner. Read through each of them and react to the one(s) that open windows for you. Each life is unique, and the priming questions impact each of us differently.

SENSITIZING QUESTIONS AND PROMPTS

1. There are "firsts," "lasts," and perhaps "always" things for the holiday and special occasions. What fits into each category for you? Would you add other possibilities — maybe, I wish, could be, if only, later, never, or more?

2. What firsts would you most want to bring to this holiday season? What lasts would be positive for you — those you would be happy never to revisit and those that will cause you to experience loss when they are no more?

3. Who, what people might be in the first and the last categories?

4. What might be the first and last possibilities?

5. If you think about "waiting" to add or delete something from your plans, does waiting make sense now, or should waiting be eliminated from your mindset?

6. Who celebrates the holidays or occasions well? What does that person have to teach you? Who is the teacher who has a holiday or special occasion you want no part of?

7. For the person with longings — do you feel as if something is not okay with you that you struggle with being satisfied, or is it good that you are always striving? How could you plan this holiday to feel complete and be satisfied with your choices? Would you need to amend your expectations, fears, and doubts and add others? What does the always upbeat person offer you by making this season or occasion what you want?

8. For the regularly upbeat person — do you feel as if you have life figured out as if you are above it all and want to stay there? Is there any longing for something more or other? When you see people who are more of what you are — more upbeat, or maybe detached from reality in that they only see the good or something else — do you say, yes, I want more of that, or do you say, deal with reality with me, or somewhere in between? What does that tell you? What does the person with longings have to offer you by making this holiday or occasion what you want?

9. If you bravely were to add in three new "firsts", what would they be? What three things would you want to end?

10. For some people, an important part of the holidays is saying to those around them what they have to say. People send cards, write letters, give presents, and entertain. For this year, if you are genuinely being frank with yourself, what would you do, eliminate, amend, or never do again, if anything? For this year, what would you add, expand, amend, or want to be part of your rituals going forward?

11. Many people spend time with family for the holidays. Who is your actual family, your intended, that is, by choice family? Who thinks they are in your inner circle? Who is in your inner circle? Who is good for you and how come? Do you want to make a point to tell them?

12. Many people have full lives all year. If you were going to make the last month of the year something different, unique, unusual, unexpected, other than your usual life, for the first time, or for the last time, what would you do, not do, not say, not say?

13. If this is the last time of something, how can you make sure that you are as fully present for it as you want to be? If this is the first time for something, how much will you allow yourself to be outside your comfort zone?

14. Do you lead with the positives, seeing yourself in the best light? Do you lead with the negatives about yourself, being highly critical? What if, for a first or last, you reversed what you do?

15. What words perfectly describe the holiday you want to create this year?

HAPPY BIRTHDAY: THE REAL, THE REMEMBERED, THE HOPED FOR

Birthdays are important to most of us. Our "birth-day" is ours and not shared with most other people. When you meet someone with the same birth date, it can feel as if there is an affinity, something shared. Celebrating birthdays in some families are grand events from childhood—a huge craft party with a dozen stations for a very happy ten-year-old; for her Mother, a catered dinner with formal wear for a 50th birthday, or a trip to Tahiti for a milestone birthday. In other families, a gathering with a cake suffices. Then, of course, there are places where birthdays come and go with little to no notice. A nonprofit organization in my community bakes custom birthday cakes for any child who does not get one any other way; the child gets to pick exactly what they want. Like many things, birthdays get imbued with meaning. What does Happy Birthday mean to you?

Ask yourself each question offered. Consider responding to a question(s) that makes you smile, that you are attracted to answering, and to one or two you don't like or want to turn away from. Facing what you don't like, or are uncomfortable with, is often a path to the most significant learning. These questions are guides to prime or stimulate your memories and thoughts about your life. The questions are not intended to be answered in a literal manner. Read through each of them and react to the one(s) that open windows for you. Each life is unique, and the priming questions impact each of us differently.

SENSITIZING QUESTIONS AND PROMPTS

1. Happy Birthday to you! What are your first thoughts, feelings, and memories? Who was part of those times? Who was missing? Whom did you wish might have been there but was not—because of death, divorce, lack of interest, being in the military, they just did not show up, or more?

2. What did your parents or caregivers think about birthdays? What did they teach you?

3. What elements make a birthday a celebration? What are things to avoid—no chores, no schoolwork, nothing you don't want to do?

4. What did you offer to your children, friend, or partner along the way to honor their birthday?

5. Can you recall a birthday that was just right, just what you wanted; it may even make you smile now. Can you remember a birthday that was especially or painfully disappointing? What happened? What do you recall about how that was for you?

6. Is there any trauma in your life associated with birthdays? What was it, and how does that impact your life now if it does? What have you done, over the years, to handle those experiences? Is there more to do?

7. What is your idea of the "perfect" birthday for you or someone else?

8. Surprises at birthday time are often offered. For some of us, that is joyful and pleasant. For others, being surprised is upsetting and uncomfortable. Where are you on that continuum, and what do you know about that for you? Do the people around you know if you like surprises or not? Do you want to tell them if they don't know?

9. If you were ill on a particular birthday or birthdays, even in the hospital, how has that impacted your life then and now as you think about that experience?

10. Do you long for a particular way to celebrate your birthday, your child's, your partner, or friend, or is this part of life of little consequence to you?

11. What do you wish for on your birthday?

12. If you do not want to be the center of attention on your birthday or at any time, how do you mitigate that feeling with what other people who care about you want to do?

13. Is celebrating birthdays vital to you? As you age, have they gotten more or less important? What is there to learn from that evolution?

14. Do you know the birthday preferences of the people around you and try to deliver on them, or do you think whatever you offer should be successful?

15. Have you experienced conflict within yourself or between you and someone else about a birthday? What did you take away from that experience? On reflection, what is there to know now?

16. Are there other days of the year and times of your life that are more important than birthdays—anniversaries, milestone dates—that you prefer to celebrate?

17. If you don't like birthdays and someone important to you does, how do you navigate the differences?

18. Is one just right birthday enough, or do you desire your birthday to be significant each year? Should it last a day, a week, or a month? Is that expectation true for you with your children, friend, partner, or parents?

19. Is it better for you to give or receive on your birthday?

Happy Birthday to you!

UNCOVERING TREASURES THAT MATTER: A PERSON. AN EXPERIENCE. A THING.

Perhaps this is the basic idea or focus of our lives. Of course, there are other things to attend, handle, manage, experience, and do. However, tuning into what matters is essential to having a good life. A treasure can be a person, an experience, a thing; it can be tiny, large, or enormous. It can be brief and ongoing. It can be something or someone we knew was significant at the moment or not. A treasure. What is a treasure?

A treasure – a person, an experience, a thing — something cherished, valued, prized, honored, significant, life-altering, meaningful, valuable in a monetary sense, an emotional understanding, or otherwise. Paying attention to, noticing, focusing energy on, preserving, honoring, noting, and resting with awareness are some ways to celebrate a treasure.

Sometimes we take a treasure for granted until it is gone. Sometimes we know this person, experience or thing will be savored for all time. These treasures can be part of our legacy, our private and most personal thoughts or memories, our secrets never to be revealed, or they can be things to be shouted from the rooftop, enshrined, touted, shared, and revered. Of course, as always, all the choices are good. The challenge is always to see, find, discover, know, what and who we want to be and celebrate in this life.

Ask yourself each question offered. Consider responding to a question(s) that makes you smile, that you are attracted to answering, and to one or two you don't like or want to turn away from. Facing what you don't like, or are uncomfortable with, is often a path to the most significant learning. These questions are guides to prime or stimulate your memories and thoughts about your life. The questions are not intended to be answered in a literal manner. Read through each of them and react to the one(s) that open windows for you. Each life is unique, and the priming questions impact each of us differently.

SENSITIZING QUESTIONS AND PROMPTS

1. What are your favorite treasures? Choose one. Make a list. Sort. Sift. Collect them all. See what you see.

2. Are your treasures a person or people? An experience or experiences? A thing?

3. What criteria do you use to put something on a treasure list?

4. Does something that is treasured need to be positive? Can people, experiences, or things that were negative, scary, uncomfortable, or embarrassing be treasured, too? For example, can something or someone who shaped your path in life — pulling you toward or away from where you were headed — be treasured and significant?

5. If you are going to describe in exquisite detail what that treasure is, what matters to you to include?

6. If you are going to acknowledge and write about a treasured thing that matters, would you say something like: what it is, where you got it, how much it cost, why it has meaning, and who you would want to have it if you were to give it away or had to give it away, and what meaning would you want them to understand is embedded in it for you?

7. If you are going to acknowledge and write about a treasured *person*, you might say,

   ✓ Where you met — e.g., at birth, at the grocery store, etc.

   ✓ When you knew that person mattered — as specifically as you can recall when that awakened sense of the meaning of that person came to you if you know

   ✓ Why they are they so important, significant, and impactful to you

   ✓ If you were to tell them, what would you say? Have you told them what they have brought you and your life along the way?

   ✓ Now that you have noticed, written, and acknowledged this person in your mind, heart, and soul, what is different for you than before this awareness?

If you are going to acknowledge and write about a treasured *experience*, would you say:

   ✓ What happened?

   ✓ Where were you physically, emotionally, and mentally when you had the experience?

   ✓ Did you understand its import at the time?

   ✓ If not, what enhanced its value later?

   ✓ What was significant about the experience — the specific detail(s) that has riveted this time in your mind and heart?

   ✓ As you focus, remember, re-experience what happened; what do you see now that maybe was not apparent at the time of the experience or along the way, as you held it inside of you without reviewing it?

   ✓ Do you want to tell anyone about it, share it? If so, to whom and why? If not, is it meaningful to you to do something active with it — such as write it down, save it for a day, week, however long and then tear it up, burn it, toss it?

Each of us has treasured *things* we hold on to and value. If you wish, you may also bring your treasured item or a photograph of it, to show as you read.

   ✓ Describe the object, where, when, and from whom.

   ✓ How did you feel, and what was your first thought when you saw it, brought it home, and used it for the first time?

   ✓ What is it that makes it special for you? What is its value — sentimental, financial, other?

   ✓ Does it symbolize something for you?

   ✓ How would it affect you? How would your life be different if you never had it or lost it?

   ✓ Do you have any new revelations when thinking and writing about this object, such as new thinking that may not have occurred to you before giving it this time and attention?

✓ Is there someone you would like to give this object to now or at some future time? Now or later? Why that person?

For example, I have a beaded bracelet I made from the beaded necklaces my Mother left behind. The bracelet has some value in itself, but its most important worth is the memories I have of seeing my Mother wearing those beads. I have a particular person in mind who, I believe, would value the bracelet as much as I do. I will give it to her when the time is right.

8. All experiences, even treasured ones, do not need to be shared. What is the most challenging thing you have dealt with that has impacted your life? e.g., my Father's watch and what it brings to me as I remember the good he brought me along with the rest of the story.

9. Who is the most difficult person you have encountered that has had a treasured and significant impact on your life? e.g., the romantic partnership that did not work out but taught you one or two or three or more of the most important things you now know.

10. What is the most challenging experience you have lived with, and which has had a treasured impact on your life?

11. As you have taken stock of *Treasures That Matter*, specifically about a person, experience, or a thing, what do you notice about yourself? What surprises you? What is confirmed for you?

CATEGORY X

WHAT IS AHEAD? WHERE TO?

Legacy – Legacy Letter

Who Are You, and What Do You Value?

The Toasts You Want To Hear

If Not Now, When?

What I Know To Be So

Where Are You Going in Your Life and How Will You Get There?

What Matters? Now What?

What happens as you think about your future self? This is a part of your life when there may be questions to answer about generativity, that is, what do you want to offer to people who matter to you? Is there more for you? Do you need, have, or want a bucket list? Do you turn away from even the notion of a bucket list and want to let the days unfold, choosing or letting life happen? For some people, planning is essential to the good life. For others, not so much. What are the stories to tell? What matters now?

LEGACY – LEGACY LETTER
WHO ARE YOU AND WHAT DO YOU VALUE?
THE TOASTS YOU WANT TO HEAR

Legacy is a definition — what you do now, have done, created, contributed to, and the result of being here and living a full life. There are many definitions of legacy. We often think of it as something that continues after we no longer do whatever we did—whether because we have died, that experience ended, or we have moved to a different phase of life (such as child-rearing). Legacy also relates to the choices we make each day. What gets our time, attention, focus, energy, involvement, and concern speaks to what we bring to this life, our legacy. Whether you choose to look at legacy as what you will leave when you stop doing what you have done or cannot do what you have done, your legacy at death, or the legacy of your ongoing choices, consider the result, what exists after you have done what you have done and, what that means to you.

If you intend to create a legacy, to impact the world, your world, or particular people, you might imagine why that legacy has meaning for you. Becoming conscious of your legacy and its current importance can provide your life with meaning and clarity

Perhaps, writing a legacy letter to the people you care about and who care about you is your preferred choice. That letter can change and be updated. A legacy letter is a way to share your values, blessings, contributions, traditions, life's lessons, hopes and dreams for the future, love, and forgiveness with your family, friends, and community. Whether you are part of a family, have friends, or a community, there are people whom you impact and are affected by what you do and who you are. A legacy letter is an updated 3,500-year-old tradition that can be "a loving document that translates your personal and family stories and values into life lessons that can inform and transform the younger generation."

Ask yourself each question offered. Consider responding to a question(s) that makes you smile, that you are attracted to answering, and to one or two you don't like or want to turn away from. Facing what you don't like, or are uncomfortable with, is often a path to the most significant learning. These questions are guides to prime or stimulate your memories and thoughts about your life. The questions are not intended to be answered in a literal manner. Read through each of them and react to the one(s) that open windows for you. Each life is unique, and the priming questions impact each of us differently.

SENSITIZING QUESTIONS AND PROMPTS

1. Today, are you drawn to writing a legacy letter, creating a legacy statement for yourself, or something else? What motivates you in one direction or the other? If you chose one for today, do you want to create some reminder for yourself to do the other at another time

2. What does legacy mean to you? Is it the same as life purpose? Is it different? How so? Does that matter?

3. If you were to write a few lines about what legacy you want or have created, what would they be?

4. If you imagine who might be impacted by your legacy, who is that person or those people? How is that awareness for you? Are there still gaps if there are many people, a broad and full list? Is it okay if it is narrow and limited, or do you want or need to do something about that awareness? What would that be? What would you do?

5. Legacy can be many different things: values, life lessons, essential memories or experiences or stories, wishes for others, hopes of what your being here has brought to the world, and more. What three main items do you want to highlight as you look at your legacy? What are you eliminating as less important than those three? As you look at this list, are you okay with them? Surprised? Disappointed? Something else? Is a revision of those priorities for you now?

6. Why does it matter to look at the question of legacy?

7. Do you understand and appreciate the legacy of the people who have lived before you or are important to you in your current life? Who were those important people — family members, neighbors, a scout leader, a church or synagogue person, a friend, or even a momentary connection with a stranger?

8. Would it be meaningful to you to ask someone you know to listen to your statement of legacy? If so, whom, and why that person? When will you do that? Would you ask them to write something to share with you, too?

9. Are there parts of your legacy or history that you want to repair, resolve, heal, or clean up? What are they? Will you do that repair, healing, cleaning up? If not, how come? If so, when?

10. Does legacy imply assets and money to you? If so, to whom do you want to give what? You can often include with trust documents who might get particular things, including stories, objects, treasures, or a bequest beyond what is covered in trust documents. Some examples, if you have children, do you want a child to have a particular photograph with the accompanying story? Or do you want a beloved friend to get something specific, with or without financial value, that you had not thought about doing until now? What would be on such a list? Would it make sense to create that list now and then have a system for updating it?

11. When you think of the concept of legacy, what feelings do you have?

12. If you choose to do something today, you are choosing not to do some other things. Are you making choiceful selections or instinctive or automatic selections? Are you choosing to do what you have always done, learned from what you watched your family do, or are you thinking about who and what you want and need to be? How do those choices impact your legacy?

13. Some people prefer to live in the present and not think beyond that reality. Is that okay? Not, okay? What are the good things about that way of being? What are the challenges? Is there a growth edge here for you?

14. Some people live in the past or the future. Is that okay? Not, okay? What are the good things about that way of being? What are the challenges? Is there a growth edge here for you?

15. Are there people in your life whom you know personally or from a distance who are models of how you want your legacy to be? Who are they, and what do they model for you?

16. Sometimes, people say, even as adults, "I want to be like you when I grow up." If you have had that experience, what is there to learn from that? Who was or is that person, and what do they bring you? If you have not had that experience but consider the question now, is there someone who models for you things that you want to have as part of your legacy?

17. What legacy did you receive from your parents? Good? Bad? A mixture?

18. Who else in your life has influenced your ideas of legacy?

19. In a legacy letter, what would you say: life lessons? Mistakes and what you have learned? Observations? Contributions? Achievements? Adventures? Liaisons? Favorite recipes? Apologies? Expressions of grievances unsaid until you write that letter? Love to someone who never knew you loved them? Love to someone who knew you loved them but not how much? A challenging experience? What else?

20. Whom would you want to read your legacy letter, and on what occasion? Are there people you would put on a list to receive your letter? When should they get it? At death? A year after you die? Five years later? How come?

21. What are three questions or filters you have for yourself that may expand, enhance, or alter your daily choices in a way that will contribute to the legacy you want to leave at the end of your life?

22. What and with whom would it be good for you to heal, repair, end, change, and have the life you want to create the best legacy?

23. Are there people you would ask to write a legacy letter so you could have it when they are no longer with you, by death, by choice, by circumstance?

24. Is legacy a concept only to consider if you are older? Is legacy a good concept anchoring when you are mid-life even though we know we don't know what mid-life is?

IF NOT NOW, WHEN?

Life moves along at its own pace. We turn toward awareness or away from it, sometimes one and sometimes the other. We each have a propensity to do one or the other. If you wish, take time to consider; if Not Now, When? That could mean you might say to someone that you care about them, even love them, something you have been hesitant to say for, let's assume, good reason. That could mean you walk away from a goal you held for a long time, but it does not belong to you now that you have permitted yourself to let it go. Think about it Now. Write about how the question might move you in a new, unexpected, delayed, or scary direction.

On this occasion, please write no more than 250 words.

WHAT I KNOW TO BE SO

Things you have learned. Items you have been taught. What have your experiences been? What you observe. What you wish you knew as a child, as a young adult, someone new to—relationships, parenting, working, facing illness, aging, and more. What we know to be so fundamentally impacts everything we do, say, think, feel, and believe every day. Because we attend to things that are congruent with our interior lives, we find reinforcement in that knowing. Most of us, most of the time, avoid placing ourselves in dissonant situations. We know what we know. Sometimes we forget what we know. Sometimes we ignore what we know. Sometimes we know what we know and are self-righteous about that knowing. Sometimes we are confused because at that moment, what we know is being challenged, or we are coming upon something novel.

What I know to be so. We know things, feel things, and collect sensations or memories or stuff within us. The threads that hold our consciousness together are something strong, clear, and well known. Other times, there are things we know to be so, which have come to us in less known ways. How they shape our experience of what we do, with whom we do whatever, what we turn towards and what we turn away from are all critical to having the life we have. If you pause and see what you know to be so, there is a chance to review, reflect, let go of, strengthen, and face reality. Life continues if we do and do and do without pausing. What remains may not be the life we could have, the life we more clearly chose, had we looked head-on at what we know to be so.

If you stop, even for a few moments, and see what you know to be so, this may be a time for something more or different that is just right for you, better for you, more expressive and reflective of whom you have become knowingly and unconsciously too.

Time to reinforce what you know to be so? Time to reconsider what you thought to be so?

Ask yourself each question offered. Consider responding to a question(s) that makes you smile, that you are attracted to answering, and to one or two you don't like or want to turn away from. Facing what you don't like, or are uncomfortable with, is often a path to the most significant learning. These questions are guides to prime or stimulate your memories and thoughts about your life. The questions are not intended to be answered in a literal manner. Read through each of them and react to the one(s) that open windows for you. Each life is unique, and the priming questions impact each of us differently.

SENSITIZING QUESTIONS AND PROMPTS

1. What do you know to be so? What are ten or more important things you know to be so?

2. How do you know what you know to be so? How do you know what you don't know that you think is so?

3. Are there secret things you know but don't want to know? Or are there things you know you wouldn't want to tell anyone else? What are they? How come you don't want to tell anyone else?

4. Does knowing what you know to be so give you comfort, satisfaction, worry, fear, or something else?

5. What do you know today that you didn't know yesterday? How did you come to know what that new knowing is?

6. What did you know yesterday that you did not know the day before? How did you come to know what that new knowing is? How is that for you if you haven't learned anything new today or yesterday? What might you do differently tomorrow, so you know something new tomorrow from what you know today?

7. What do you wish you knew when you were younger? When was that? How would your life have been different if you knew then what you know now?

8. Who were your teachers? Who are your teachers? Do you need another teacher now? How would you find that person or people?

9. Are there things you know that you wish you did not know? What is there to do about that?

10. Among the things you know to be so, what is most important?

11. If you were to be defined by what you know is so, how would you want people to know you? If you were to be defined by what you know is so, what would you never want people to know about you? For example. If you know that most people are good, you might want people to think that you see the best in people; you might not want people to think you were naive or unable to discern.

12. In what way(s) does chronicling what you know to be so serve you? And, in what way(s) is that limiting, if at all?

13. If your goal was to challenge each or some of the things you know to be so, where would you start? Do you think it is a good idea to question what you know to be so?

14. If you want to teach or suggest or offer to younger people—students, your children, your friends— what you know to be so, how would you go about doing that? How would you want that to impact them?

15. Is your fundamental approach to life being a teacher or student? Are there some situations with some kinds of people where you are one or the other? Would someone who knows you well concur with your assessment? You might want to ask them.

16. For the person who is most frequently the teacher, what needs are being met inside of you by offering what you know to be so? What are the positive and the other needs being met?

17. For the person who is most frequently the student, what needs are being met inside of you by receiving what you want to know? What are the positive and the other needs being met?

18. When you are primarily the teacher, how is it for you if someone does not want to be your student, especially if you offer what you know to be positive, helpful, useful, and kind?

19. When you are primarily the student, how is it for you if someone does not want to be your teacher, help you out when you truly need and want access to know what they know to be so?

20. What does that mean when others validate something you know to be so? When others discount something you know to be true, what does that mean to you?

21. If you were going to organize your life around the key things that you know are so, what would they be?

22. How do you handle competing thoughts about what you have held dear, true? Do you discount them? Forget them? Ignore them? What else?

23. Can you be pals with someone with whom what you know to be so is mostly different from what they know to be so? How do you manage those differences?

24. What if someone else knows what you know to be so? Is that always good when you find someone like that? What could be the downside if there is one?

25. If your partner, grown child, important friend wants to know what you know, do you tell them? If the answer is, "of course," would there or could there be a circumstance when you would not tell them?

26. If you fall in love, do you need that what you know to be so gets shared? How come?

27. Is there a legacy to be created of what you know to be so? To whom would you offer or present what you know to be so? Are there people you would not tell?

28. Would it be good for you to systematically check in with yourself on what you know to be so? How would you do that? Why do that or why not do that?

29. Why is there value in collecting what you know to be so if there is? Is there a downside?

30. What did your Mother or Father know to be so? Their parents?

31. Is it helpful to think about what others know to be so? How come?

32. If you look around where you have spent time now or in the past, what do you know about the people with whom you interact(ed)? Do you let yourself see the truth of what is there? Do you deny reality? How come? How does that take care of you—by seeing what is or by ignoring/denying what is? Does it take care of you?

33. If you truly know what you know and you do not like what you know to be so, then what? Can you turn toward that knowing fully and openly and face the truth? If not, what is the price you are paying?

34. If you truly know what you know and you like what you know to be so, is there another step forward to making your life richer, better, or more?

35. Knowing what you know to be so can be good, challenging, scary, and many other things. What is this process of discovery like for you right this moment?

36. If after reading these prompts, you have one thought or feeling or idea or sensation that has come to you that was not there before, what is it? Now, what do you do with that awareness?

WHERE ARE YOU GOING IN YOUR LIFE AND HOW WILL YOU GET THERE?

As you approach each new day, there are possibilities. Many of us go about our days in a routine way, doing what we have planned or, for a few among us, letting what comes come. Few people actually choose how to spend their most important resource, time. If you consider where you are going in your life, perhaps you have an idea of the next thing — the goal, the trip, the question you are trying to answer, the requirement, the need. Imagine, though, where you are going. Then, imagine what belief or focus or way of being or sense of yourself that is important to you, may help as you select what is good and right for you as you move forward.

You may be in decision making mode about something, survival mode, creative mode, reflecting mode, soothing or healing mode, completion mode, searching mode, sorting mode, or have some other way of looking at the question, where are you going. "Going" may not be what you are considering at all. Being, pausing, or staying still could be where you are just now. Take some time to see what is happening to, for, and within you. Remember, you may have an idea of where you are going, and your psyche may have another idea for you. Being open to what your inner wisdom brings and offers to you is the way to the truest life, a life that is yours alone.

Then, imagine how to get where you want to go. Consider what seems possible and what seems impossible that will open your heart, head, body, and soul. Let in more than you ever thought might be real for you. Really.

Ask yourself each question offered. Consider responding to a question(s) that makes you smile, that you are attracted to answering, and to one or two you don't like or want to turn away from. Facing what you don't like, or are uncomfortable with, is often a path to the most significant learning. These questions are guides to prime or stimulate your memories and thoughts about your life. The questions are not intended to be answered in a literal manner. Read through each of them and react to the one(s) that open windows for you. Each life is unique, and the priming questions impact each of us differently.

SENSITIZING QUESTIONS AND PROMPTS

1. Where are you going? How do you know? Is that right for you? Who says? Are you choosing consciously, or unconsciously, actively, or passively? Have you always been on this path?

2. Are there competing voices or ideas inside of you that suggest you consider something else? Do your dreams challenge what you are doing or support what you are doing?

3. What dreams do you have? If none, are you asking for dreams to help guide you? Do you want to ask for dreams to help augment what you think about and know about your life?

4. The proverbial question is, if you look back at your life from some time in the future, what will you see and is that what you want to see?

5. What would you not let yourself consider doing, choosing? What are the thoughts, ideas, and places you might go that are taboo even to consider? How come? Has your breathing changed as you even imagine those possibilities?

6. Are there people in your world who support where you are going? Who are they? Are there people in your world saying you might consider going elsewhere? What is their message to you? Are there people in your world who discourage you, directly or indirectly? What are the implications of that awareness?

7. Can you name those limits if you can see limits in your life — because of health, money, time, fears, doubts, self-definition, whatever? Can you find a way to create a counterpoint to each limit?

8. Is where you are going consistent with how you have always thought about your life? If so, is that okay? If this direction is new? How did it come to you? Did the direction come from outside of you or inside of you? Do you own it as a good thing for you now?

9. If you challenge yourself and say, what is 180 degrees from here — the exact opposite from where I am headed, what would that be? Would that be worthwhile to consider? Is there even a tiny piece of that opposite worthwhile adding to your current and future life? For example, if you are a traveler, would it be helpful to stay at home and fully notice what is there, or .... If you are creating something, would it be beneficial to savor what is, or…If you are winding down, would it be helpful to wind up for, or…?

10. Who helps you get where you are going? Who impedes you from getting to where you are going? Do you need more help from others? How will you find them?

11. Perhaps if you notice more carefully, there are people you already know who can help you move forward if you turn toward them. Are the regular people in your life filling your time but not giving you what you need to move forward? Do you need more challenges? Do you need less challenge? How can you ask for what would help you?

12. What three things support "getting there" wherever there is? What are three things that inhibit or distract or disrupt or interfere with your "getting there" wherever there is? Now what?

13. Today, write an action plan to help you get where you are going — including a vision board, talking, and thinking. What else might support your process? Who else can nudge or encourage or clarify and help move you along? Whom should you avoid?

14. Being brutally honest with yourself, what is good for you? What is not? Who is good for you? Who is not?

15. The obstacles to going where we want are subtle and not. What are the subtle barriers, limiting factors, and inhibiting elements that hinder you from being who you truly are? Now what?

16. If you find yourself looking away from a possibility, what does that turning away offer by way of learning?

17. If you are relaxed and peaceful because you know where you are going, how can you celebrate that knowing?

18. How can you remember if you are comfortable with how you will move forward in your life?

19. Letting questions stimulate, stir, challenge, and move you to a more conscious life that incorporates your inner wisdom is an ongoing process. How will you continue your access to your awareness?

WHAT MATTERS? NOW WHAT?

There are many lists of personal values—sort among the values important to you at this time of your life. Sort the values into most important, important, and least important. Then sort them a second time or more until you end up with three to five of the most important values to you now and for what is ahead in your life.

Your values + your behavior = success. Success in life is when your behavior/what you do, don't, say, or don't say matches your values.

Consider. Act. Be still. Breathe. Imagine. Pause. Then write about your values.

SENSITIZING QUESTIONS AND PROMPTS

1. Take each value of the three to five you have chosen and do the following:

   - Define the essence of this value as you consider it. What does it mean to you?
   - Write about the competing, contrary voices in your head about this value.
   - For each value, complete the following sentence stem.

     "As I look at this important value to me, something I see more clearly about why this value is important to me is …."

   - One by one, be sure to write an awareness for each of them.

2. Magic. If you woke up tomorrow and were living the values you chose, what would be different than is true today? What new choices would you make, intensify, or expand? Or what choices would you stop making, alter, or refine?

3. What behavior(s) must you add to your life to live your values and the life you want and need?

4. What would be different from before this review, this values sort? What would be the same?

5. Who in your life would support this new way of being? Who would challenge any changes? Who would reject you and the changes you want to make? What are the implications of those outcomes for you?

6. After taking each step, complete the sentence stem, "What comes up for me now is…

7. If these values matter to you, what are your unexpected choice? What and whom do you need to help you move forward on this path? How will you assess if you are moving forward and in ways that are productive and meaningful for you?

8. When will you do what needs to be done to live the life that matters?

9. How will you remember what you want to remember?

Part Four:
APPENDICES

CONTENTS

FINDING CLIENTS: THE NECESSARY EFFORT FOR ALL YOUR CLINICAL WORK, MADE EASIER

MARKETING AND PROMOTION: SELLING ONE'S SERVICES. LOCATING PARTICIPANTS

Oh no. I can't do that. I don't want to do that. That is bad, not my strength, not what I went to graduate school to do. It is crass. It diminishes me. And more.

> **Many therapists find the idea of marketing an anathema or repugnant. And yet, you, my colleague, have something profoundly meaningful and helpful to offer.**

Some potential clients know that therapy has life-altering possibilities. Many potential clients do not know what therapy of any kind can offer. Only you can tell them. Really. Only you can tell them or another well-trained and experienced therapist.

In addition, many therapists think or feel or believe, somewhere on that continuum, that offering a group, any group, is hard, more challenging to do than seeing an individual client, may not be worth the effort financially, and they may not think they have the skills to do so.

> **Without selling or saying anything beyond what you know to be true, part of our responsibility is to teach people what we have to offer.**

As is valid with any clinical work you offer, there are many ways to gather clients into your practice. The same is true for workshops. The most typical ways you might begin to find participants include:

- Asking your existing clients if that is appropriate and acceptable

- Telling your referral sources what you are going to do and asking them to refer to you

- Sending notices to your professional community about the value of this workshop and reminding them you will send people back to their practices after the workshop

- Offering a workshop experience for other therapists who may benefit from writing and reading their stories to other therapists in a safe environment

- Talking to physicians who serve the kind of client you want to treat about what you are doing and asking them to tell their patients about your workshop

Marketing is its own topic. I encourage you to think about marketing as giving people the gift of knowing more about something they may find valuable, i.e., your services, your skills.

> One particularly effective way of marketing a workshop has been to offer a free, short workshop at a professional meeting of your peers, or to a group of therapists you know, or even to people in your church/synagogue, etc. Typically, the theme, "Uncovering Treasures That Matter: A person, an experience, a thing," is the topic to use.

It is therapeutic, and since you are a therapist, it can lead to therapy. Divide the audience into small groups (or dyads if only a few people come) and ask them to write about a treasure that matters to them — a person, an experience, a thing — write about it in any way they choose, then read it to the others in their small group. They will respond with support and have an energizing moment that will often lead to an interest in going forward. Give this group experience away for free.

For several reasons, the one-day workshop option has many advantages over asking people to sign up for five weeks in sequence or ten weeks, etc. Because many adults have busy lives, committing to a regular weekly schedule is challenging. The expectation that each person will write on an identified theme each week requires a significant commitment of time and energy. While there are clear advantages to the sense of community and intimacy developed when meeting with the same people over multiple weeks, some of the connectivity can also be developed in an alternative model. That is, monthly or every other month one-day workshops where participants can come again and again, as they are able and are interested in a particular theme being considered. Over time, a community of people can be formed in this ad hoc way and produce an enhanced sense of well-being by having people know and care about each other.

In addition, finding participants is made more accessible by asking for a one-day commitment. Once they have the experience, almost everyone returns for another or many other workshops.

The therapy process can be deepened by having more time between sessions to do further writing on the theme, meet with their therapist individually, do other self-development, or pause to reflect.

> **People get to choose the themes of greater significance and value to them.**

THE TTM METHOD FOR SPECIFIC POPULATIONS

As a clinician, Bonnie has offered TTM workshops to her psychotherapy patients and other adults seeking psychological growth and reprocessing their lives. She has also provided workshops to groups of psychotherapists, physicians, synagogue/church groups, a group of artists, teachers and professors, airline personnel, tech groups, and assorted groupings of people searching for more depth or understanding in their lives.

> The stunning thing about this material is that it can be used
> in widely diverse groups and by a range of leaders.

Certainly, each clinician will offer a distinct experience based on your training, experience, and supervision. Ethically, what you bring to the time spent with the people who join your groups will be enhanced by your extensive knowledge of what can be helpful. A TTM group that is both therapeutic and therapy, while different from a process group, can provide a way to help patients or clients know, differentiate, and be able to handle their feelings and thoughts in an expanded, in-depth manner.

One target audience for the workshops is those whom Medicare covers. As an aside, helping to get services to people over 65 was the initial motivating factor for writing this book; as any clinician knows, being a Medicare provider is a choice and one that too few clinical people choose to meet the need. Some say the Medicare system is easy to access and from which to receive payments. Other people see the system as daunting.

Medicare covers every person when they turn 65 and beyond unless they continue to have insurance coverage through an employer. Mental health services are a covered expense if offered by a Medicare provider and offered to a person with a mental health diagnosis. The diagnosis can be an adjustment disorder, generalized anxiety disorder, depression, and more. Many people 65+ have a legitimate mental health need for clinical services. Currently, roughly 10,000 people turn 65 each day, and approximately 12,000 people will turn 65 each day within the next ten years. That means that as the number of people who could access low-cost or no-cost mental health services through Medicare increases, the gap between how many providers are available and the service needs for the 65+ population also increases. More people are eligible for services. They need them. The number of providers is inadequate.

The solution! Run a group with Medicare covered patients, all of whom have some mental health diagnosis.

In that case, this is a cost-effective way to offer a valuable, evidence-based, clinically substantial treatment protocol to an underserved population and get paid, making it cost-effective. Everyone receives something of outstanding value—therapeutic help, community building, legacy, increased well-being, and the therapist gets paid for their work product.

Time to start your first group!

Everything you need is provided between the covers of this book!

We believe you will be hooked on offering clinical services with this method after a one-start trial!

CHOOSING A RELEVANT THEME FOR THE INDIVIDUAL CLIENT OR A COUPLE

As a therapist with clinical training and instincts, this question and its answer may seem obvious or daunting. Sometimes, the client says the exact words that a theme suggests. "My birthday is next Friday. I have never had a birthday party or a birthday cake." There is a theme— "Happy Birthday: The Real, The Remembered, The Hoped For." If there is a question of which of several themes would be better, just check out the prompts and choose or offer them both to the client and see where their inner wisdom takes them and what they select to address.

Sometimes, there is angst and distress, pain, and sadness, with an identifiable reason—a transition such as a divorce, loss of previously good health, or getting fired from a job. There is a specific theme to offer them and the possibility of something broader.

Frequently, as a way to gently introduce the TTM method, offer the theme of "Uncovering Treasures That Matter—a person, an experience, a thing." This theme, which most clients find easy to think and write about. Offers tremendous value and eases them into this writing method. When we write about something of significance to us, rarely is it a waste. I cannot imagine that being the case; our clients just wouldn't do it. The "Uncovering Treasures That Matter" theme is broadly successful and honored in a way that may seem obvious, but most people never ever write about what is important to them. They think they will and want to say, "Soon, I am going to write about that thing that matters so much to me." It just does not happen.

> **You, the therapist, has a profound and consequential gift to offer to your clients with just this one theme, "Uncovering Treasures That Matter."**

And, of course, there are so many more.

Truthfully, the choice of the theme and prompts comes from many factors, primarily your therapeutic intuition, the nuance, your best guess, or something inside of you that just says; this idea would be helpful. Since clients willing to write will interpret the questions in a way and direction that honors them and what they need, no matter what theme you offer or what prompt they choose, their writing will lead them forward. Of course, some clients will want and perhaps need more direction. Offer what you see to be the most helpful path forward.

> **The TTM writing process is a method. If there is no theme that seems just right for your client, write your own and still use the protocol.**

Tell us, and we'll put it on a list of themes to write in the future. Honestly, we think we have covered what will be helpful for 99% of the clinical issues you encounter.

The TTM method is simple and straightforward. Listen, as you surely do, to what your client is talking to you about. Having read the themes, check out what might move their process of clarity, insight, association, and connection to you, the therapist, along the path of healing.

Access to therapy is limited by the number of trained people, the cost, and the motivation to receive help. This method expands, deepens, and offers both collateral and substantive focus on a deeply personal theme chosen by you, the experienced therapist, who has been listening to what your client is saying.

> **You may feel that the words and prompts in the themes come from your own clients because that is where they came from; they came from clients in my office, groups, workshops, or couples. Their words were expanded into themes and then prompts, clinically tested to see which were most helpful, and then used in the field to make sure.**

Even when the exact words do not emerge from your client, you know, imagine, or suspect where their concern originates. If someone is having trouble getting the medical care they need, you might look at the themes of health and well-being or family of origin concerns. My client, who had learned that "If I am ill, there is something wrong with me." would not go to the emergency room with chest pains because it was so damning to her to ask for help. Of course, the writing work was only possible after she finally did go and get treatment, a painful and scary process for her.

> **You have in your hands many, many prompts to help a wide variety of clients deepen their awareness of and potential for healing around a diversity of clinical concerns we therapists face each day.**

You might go back to how you work after the client reads the material and see what happens. Sometimes a therapist's intervention hits the mark and the client shifts into their new awareness. Sometimes, of course, the client has the ah-ha moment and just gets why they do what they do or said what they said. And, sometimes, it takes a very long time to get the story that with TTM is just there for the asking with the right prompt, support, and chance to tell one's story and be witnessed. It happens almost all the time. Really.

BEING AN EFFECTIVE GROUP OR WORKSHOP LEADER

1. Allow each person to briefly reflect on what has gone on during the week, the difficulty they may have had with the assignment, and any other problems related to the group structure (but not difficulties with other group members). This helps everyone relax and become present for the session. Set a clear time limit on this check-in so everyone has a chance to have their say while preserving ample time for each group member to do their reading and receive responses from other group members later in the session.

2. *It is very easy for the conversation to wander off-topic.* It is the facilitator's responsibility to bring the group back to the subject under discussion. Use questions and gentle redirection to refocus the group. Do that multiple times if necessary.

3. *Encourage the group members to speak directly to one another and not through you,* the leader. You should not do most of the talking. If you are asked a question, turn the question back to another person in the group to respond. If you notice you are talking more than the group members, reflect on what is happening and make adjustments.

4. *Frequently remind people of the guidelines.* Feedback should be supportive. Encourage participants to point out the strengths they see in each other, and you will have the foundation for a safe group where everyone can be genuine, honest, and open with their life struggles and successes.

5. In every group, there is someone hesitant to speak up. For instance, "Susan, the experience you shared last week is very similar to what Richard has just told us. Do you have any thoughts or feelings you might want to talk about now?" If this becomes an ongoing issue, be sure to take time, in private, to talk to that group member about what you are noticing.

6. Unlike someone who does not speak, one person jumps in, takes over, and wants to run the group. You will need to contain them, so everyone has an equal time to talk. You may need to interrupt and say, "Thanks, Ted, now let's hear what the others have to say." If the behavior continues, talk to that group member privately about what you have observed.

7. Ensuring equal sharing is critical to the group leader's role. Begin and end the sessions on time. If you find the two hours insufficient to do what you want, you may need to get an agreement on extending the time, if possible.

8. *At the end of the session,* summarize what has transpired and ask each person to share a brief takeaway with the group. You could ask them to share one or two feeling words about how the session has gone for them. Then remind them of the assignment for the next session.

SCREENING FOR GROUP OR WORKSHOP PARTICIPANTS

1. Know who you are inviting into the group.

   Suppose you haven't met the person or have not had a clarifying conversation with them. In that case, you should meet with them and evaluate if the person is robust enough to follow the agreements, write about the topics, and listen to disparate viewpoints with a respectful presence and attitude.

2. Here are some detailed questions to assess potential clients:

   a. Are they within the age group relevant to this material?

   b. Do they have the physical capacity to write and read independently? If there are any limits, how will they be addressed?

   c. Will they willingly agree to the parameters of this group experience, or do they balk at your description of how this will go? Balking at the beginning is a warning signal.

   d. If the person is in therapy, ask them to check with their therapist to agree to their participation in this group experience. No exceptions. If the therapist says "no," get a signed release and talk to the therapist. Explain the purpose and process of this group and see if the therapist will agree to their participation. If the person has previously been in therapy, understand why they stopped. This may be perfectly fine or not. If they left therapy in anger, be sure to understand why. Then see if there is a potential problem to address before adding them to the group.

   e. Are there any red flags that make you concerned about their participation? Discuss your thoughts with a colleague before deciding to include that person. Rarely is this an issue, but when it occurs, it is essential to address it from the outset before having someone join the group.

GROUP OR WORKSHOP GUIDELINES

Group members must manage their behavior, particularly how they give verbal feedback to each other. Feedback in the TTM group process is defined in a distinct way, to allow each person to find their own voice and discover their own narrative. This is not a group with crosstalk, challenges, or problem-solving. This is a psycho-educational therapeutic group, not a process group. Compliance with these guidelines is a crucial component of the Uncovering Treasures That Matter protocol.

1. *Respect.* Everyone in the group is respected for who you are. No one makes disparaging comments, gestures, or nonverbal expressions. You may choose to remain quiet if you do not wish to participate in a discussion or do not feel you can be respectful in what you say. While your internal responses are your own, this group is constructed to be a safe place for each individual to explore their own stories.

2. *Active listening.* Give your full attention to the person speaking. Listen fully to what is shared. Do your best to notice and experience the person reading their story, without thinking about how you will respond. Listen with compassion and respect. Listen without judgment. Treat others with empathy, as you would wish to be treated. Affirm others by honoring different viewpoints.

3. *Compassion and encouragement.* The clear and stated intention in this group is to be positive. When you respond, speak about your own experience rather than judging, criticizing, or blaming. Avoid giving advice, criticizing, or expressing shock or judgment about what you hear. In this group, you can expect to give and receive only positive responses. In some different kinds of groups, there is a challenge and direct confrontation. This is not a group where challenge and confrontation are accepted.

4. *Self-control.* Do not interrupt or engage in conversations on the side. Be sensitive to the amount of time you talk; everyone should have a roughly equal amount of "airtime." You may find pauses uncomfortable; in this group the pauses are important. Often it is helpful to pause after someone has finished speaking to let it all sink in before responding.

5. *Nonverbal behavior.* Be careful to manage your nonverbal behavior so as not to distract or interfere with another person's reading and processing of their story. Do not, for example, leave your seat while someone is reading.

6. *"I" Statements.* Use "I" statements and speak in a way that encourages dialogue. Keep the focus on your own thoughts and feelings, do not talk about others who are not there, and be thoughtful about giving feedback. Stick to "I" or "me" statements, not "you" or "we" statements. e.g., "I had a similar experience." "I am moved by what you said." NOT, "You did what!?" If you have an emotional response to what you have heard, you might say, "When I hear you talk about _____, I feel sad, or upset, or whatever."

7. *Clarification.* Be prepared to clarify statements that others may not understand or may misinterpret. Ask the speaker to confirm your clarifying statement or restate what they wanted to say so that everyone understands the true meaning of what is shared.

GROUP OR WORKSHOP AGREEMENTS

All members of the group must understand and agree to these conditions. Go around the group and ask each person to say out loud they will abide by these agreements. While you cannot guarantee what other people will do, this verbal acknowledgment and public commitment can go a long way to increasing each participant's confidence in the safety of the group.

Confidentiality. Everything that is shared in the group stays in the group. Nothing is to be discussed with others outside the group. Someone, of course, can share their own experience about what happened in the group without talking about anyone else. This agreement provides a safe and secure place for clients to share openly. Since you cannot guarantee that each group member will honor this agreement, ask the participants to share only to their own level of comfort. This agreement is essential and absolute. You might offer examples of what works and what does not in sharing one's personal experience in the group.

Commitment to do the work. Everyone must complete all writing assignments. You will read what you wrote about the week's theme to the group. Think about what you are willing to read to the group. In the rare instance where you are unable or prefer not to read what you have written, please be sure to discuss your reluctance with the leader ahead of time and plan for how you will participate. If for some reason you are unable to write during a week, you can still come to the group, listen, and be supportive.

Commitment to attend all group sessions. It is essential to commit to attending all group sessions. If something comes up and you need to miss a session or leave early, you must let the group leader know. It is up to the leader to determine if you will have a chance to read what you had written for the session you missed later.

GROUP OR WORKSHOP TROUBLESHOOTING

As a clinician, you have your own way of working through issues. Below are some guidelines. If you still feel stuck, please get consultation. After you offer your first group, everything will get easier. And, when you do your first group, the power of this protocol and the participants' experience will be more meaningful. Once you start, you may not be able to stop!

WHAT CAN GO WRONG, AND WHAT TO DO ABOUT IT?

1. *Negative and critical comments made in the group.* Someone in the group is critical or negative about another group member. Immediately interrupt it, and stop it, when it happens. Then, at the first break, talk to the person offering the negative comments and the person who received those comments. Listen carefully to what is happening/has happened, what is being triggered or has been triggered. Decide if additional help outside the group process may be helpful or necessary for the participants. Offer that help or refer to someone else, another clinician, if that is relevant. Ask the person who was negative or judgmental if they are able and willing to abide by the agreements made. If the problem persists, you, the leader, must decide what to do. Judgmental, critical, or negative comments can totally shut down the group's positive experience. Responding to this problem *requires a careful and speedy* resolution. Help for the participant who said what they said, the receiver, and for you can be reassuring and significant. Get help for yourself if you are not clear about what to do. Do not delay!

2. *Personal discomfort when listening to the stories.* Someone in the group may get upset or destabilized by another person's writing. Ask them to hold their response until the break. Listen to the person and discover what is happening; always the first step. Look at what help the person needs—to talk to you individually once or for ongoing counseling or referral to someone else. Consider what repair may be required, depending on how the person expressed their upset. Once again, respond as quickly as possible without disrupting the group or shaming the person, but this definitely needs to be handled before the next session.

3. *Strong, dominating group member.* Someone may dominate, always need to comment, or interrupt when another person is reading their story. This must be stopped immediately, kindly, each time it occurs. The first time, gently remind the group, "Everyone gets their uninterrupted time to read their story. Please save your thoughts and comments for when the person is finished." Say this a second time if need be. On the third interruption, have a private conversation with the person and see what is happening. This has to be stopped. It will ruin the group.

4. *Lack of preparation for the group session.* One of the themes may be too hard or uncomfortable for the participant to either write about or read what they have written. Talk to that person privately and find out what the problem is. Passing on a topic is okay, one time. You can decide if you will allow the person to simply talk about the topic within their time limit. You will have to decide what to do if they do not write a second time. Obviously, you want to keep people in the group. The writing and reading are

fundamental to the experience. For example, if the person is having some difficulty writing, they may need to find a buddy to help them.

5. *Close relationships among group members.* A romance or other personal relationship may get started, which is uncomfortable or threatening to another group member. Some leaders may prefer to ask participants to delay contact outside the group until its conclusion. Since building community can be a valuable part of this experience, you, the leader, must sort out for yourself what to do. We personally do not prohibit group members from outside contact. Rather, we ask for each participant to be respectful of the impact on others. Get an agreement from each person to be independent in the group. That might mean even sitting separately. It might mean not having any whispering or other private behavior that is likely to make other people feel uncomfortable or left out. If the awareness of this developing relationship becomes an issue, you may need to discuss with the group what can be put in place to make everyone feel safer.

6. *Attendance at group sessions.* Someone may not come to the group or come late without telling you in advance. Be sure to address this right away. If this becomes a regular thing, you will have to decide whether or not that means expulsion from the group. If you decide to be loose about the time, it will likely create a range of problems. You could structure the group to start at say 10:00 a.m., but the work starts at 10:15 a.m. Being respectful to each group member is critical. Being on time is being respectful. Emphasize the agreements as you sort out who will be in the group and deal with issues promptly as they emerge!

7. *Positive or negative countertransference.* You, the clinician, may have an exceptional or uncomfortable positive feeling for or strong personal dislike to someone in the group. Since clinicians are people too, accept that this has happened and get consultation for yourself so you can do what you want and need to do in the group. Positive and negative countertransference may be your experience. Feelings happen in therapists' lives too. Get consultation.

8. *Exiting the group early.* Someone may find what goes on in the group too uncomfortable for them to continue. If someone needs to leave the group, ask them to come and say goodbye. If that is not possible or they are unwilling, ask them to write a goodbye note which you will read to the group. If they won't do either, make sure to give the group some time to talk about how the person's leaving impacts them. Either way, taking time to talk about the feelings experienced any time someone leaves the group is essential. Keep the discussion on how the participants feel and think and not a critique or evaluation of the person who has left. Remember, group safety requires the leader to manage the interactions so that each person follows the agreements made.

GROUP OR WORKSHOP FEEDBACK

The TTM process defines feedback in a distinctive way. Here are the details to be discussed with the group members:

This group is constructed to allow each person to find their own voice, their own narrative, and their own discovery. This is not a group with crosstalk, challenge, or problem-solving. This is a therapeutic group, not a process group.

1. Be respectful of each other.

2. When giving feedback to another group member, remember to be supportive and encouraging.

3. If you have an emotional response to what you have heard, you might say, "When I hear you talk about _____, I feel sad, or upset, or whatever."

4. Be careful to manage your nonverbal behavior so as not to distract or interfere with another person's reading and processing their story.

5. Avoid giving advice, criticizing, expressing shock or judgment about what you hear. In this group, you can expect to give and receive only positive responses. In some different kinds of groups, there is challenge and direct confrontation. This is not a group where challenge and confrontation are accepted.

6. While your internal responses are your own, this group is constructed to be a safe place for each individual to explore their own stories.

ETHICS AND THE LAW

INFORMED CONSENT

As a therapist, you surely have asked your clients to consent to the therapy you are offering. That is a standard of care. Since you are now offering a writing experience for some of your clients, you must decide what to do about the product produced, their written stories. As with any material a client offers you, once it becomes part of your professional record, it is discoverable. Consider how you want to handle the receipt of such material because once it is in your record, others are likely able to see it if you should get a court order or certain kinds of other legal situations. This note is not intended as legal advice. Please consult with your advisors to determine how to protect your client and you. Language you might use in your informed consent should relate to your scope of competence and in what settings you may offer this material. You may consider making sure to ask your client to keep their own writing.

CONFIDENTIALITY AND PRIVACY

We encourage you, the therapist, to help your clients make active choices about where, with whom, and if or when to share their writing and what to do with that writing. Knowing how and where a client will keep their writing private often is the difference between someone's willingness to explore fully and a short-circuited approach. Discussions about how your client wants to handle this aspect of this probing writing can be reassuring, supportive, and protective of them.

THE TAKEAWAY: CREATING A BOOK, BOOKLET, JOURNAL

Your clients who have written on the TTM life themes have worked hard to look within and uncover the treasures buried there. The collected stories are valuable and worth saving. Maybe there is a book to come, too, maybe not. There are many ways for anyone who chooses to gather together what they have written, from simply putting all the stories into one document to dropping the stories into a book template and printing copies. Here are some options available for you to discuss with your clients.

1. Create a single document: The easiest way to do this is to simply 'cut and paste' all the stories into a chronological order in one word document. Simple formatting techniques make it easy to choose a font, add page numbers, and even insert photos.

2. A title for your story: Give your story a title. Is it a drama? A comedy? An adventure story? Think about what you have written and come up with a title that fits the flow of your life. It might be helpful to check out the books and website for Six-Word Memoirs: https://www.sixwordmemoirs.com/ The challenge is to use only six words for your title, e.g. "Not Quite What I Was Planning" "In And Out Of Hot Water".

3. Creating a book: The easiest thing to do is to put all the stories into a 3-ring binder. This will keep them all together in one place. Alternatively, your clients can purchase a simple folder to hold the stories. A visit to an office supply store opens up numerous options from comb-binding, spiral binding to perfect binding to keep the printed pages together. They could be hand bound if someone is an artist. There are many possibilities.

    - Online Printing Sources: Many online sources are available for printing books. Some have templates for the writer to work with, so it is drop in the stories format. Most require the book to be in the finished format and in a PDF file for printing. It is wise to check out each of the sites first before recommending them to your clients.
    - Lulu:https://www.lulu.com/?msclkid=3b6d9e3f312d19cbbe3ac0d23ba595c7&utm_source=bing&utm_medium=cpc&utm_campaign=US%20-%20Lulu%20-%20Branded&utm_term=lulu.com%20self%20publishing&utm_content=Self-Publishing
    - Blurb: https://www.blurb.com/
    - Shutterfly: https://www.shutterfly.com/
    - UBuildABook: https://ubuildabook.com/

Assembling a book is the easy part! What matters is to celebrate and value the effort that has gone into the writing and sharing of these important stories. What comes next is up to each person—keeping their stories for themselves, sharing them with others, making a place for them as part of their legacy, writing further, or whatever wonderful possibility they can imagine!

SHARING, READING TO FAMILY MEMBERS OR OTHER IMPORTANT PEOPLE OUTSIDE THE GROUP

As is often true, the stories written are so compelling and meaningful that clients may want to read their stories to people outside the group. With the relevant caution and reminder that sharing what any group member may have said or commented about when that story was read cannot be shared, even without giving the name of the person who said what they said, of course, sharing their own stories is their choice.

SUGGESTED MEMOIR READINGS

After writing and sharing their personal stories, some clients may wish to improve their writing. Reading memoirs is one of the best ways to become a better story writer. The following is a short list of suggested books to read. Add your preferences to this list.

Angelou, Maya. *I Know Why the Caged Bird Sings*. New York: Random House, LLC. 1969.

Beah, Ishmael. *A Long Way Gone: Memoirs of a Boy Soldier*. New York: Sarah Crichton Books, 2007.

Coates, Ta-Nehisi. *Between the World and M*. New York: Spiegel & Grau, 2015.

Davis, Viola. *Finding Me: A Memoir*. New York: Harper Collins Publishers, 2022.

Didion, Joan. *The Year of Magical Thinking*. New York: Vintage Books, 2007.

Dillard, Annie. *The Writing Life*. New York: Harper & Row Publishers, Inc., 1989.

Doyle, Glennon. *Untamed*. New York: The Dial Press, 2020.

Frank, Anne. *The Diary of a Young Girl*. Edited by Otto H. Frank and Mirjam Pressler, translated by Susan Massotty, Grapevine Publishers, 1947.

Gandhi, Mahatma. *Gandhi: All Men Are Brothers, Autobiographical Reflections*. UNESCO: The Columbia University Press, 1958.

Gilbert, Elizabeth. *Eat, Pray, Love*. New York: Riverhead Books, 2006.

Greene, Graham. *A Sort of Life*. New York: Simon & Schuster, 1971.

Hong Kingston, Maxine. *The Woman Warrior: Memoirs of a Girlhood Among Ghosts*. New York: Vintage International, Random House, 1976.

Hooks, Bell. *Bone Black: Memories of Girlhood*. New York: Henry Holt and Company, 1996.

Hurston, Zora Neale. *Dust Tracks on a Road*. Philadelphia: Lippincott, 1942.

Jackson, Phil. *Sacred Hoops*. New York: Go Hachette Books, 1995.

Karr, Mary. *The Liar's Club: A Memoir*. New York: Penguin Books, 1995.

Keller, Helen. *The Story of My Life*. New York: Doubleday, 1903.

King, Stephen. *On Writing*. New York: Pocket Books Simon & Schuster, Inc., 2000.

Maathai, Wangari. *Unbowed: A Memoir*. New York: Anchor Books, 2008.

MacDonald, Helen. *H is for Hawk*. New York: Grove Press, 2014.

Martin, Steve. *Born Standing Up*. New York: Charles Scribner's & Sons, 2008.

Matthiessen, Peter. *The Snow Leopard*. London: Penguin Books, 1978.

McBride, James. *The Color of Water: A Black Man's Tribute to His White Mother.* New York: Riverhead Books, 1996.

McCourt, Frank. *Angela's Ashes*. Logan, Iowa: Perfection Learning, 1996.

Oates, Joyce Carol. *A Widow's Story*. New York: Ecco, Harper Collins, 2011.

Oliver, Mary. *Long Life: Essays and Other Writings*. Cambridge, M: De Capo Press, 2004.

Ragusa, Kym. *The Skin Between Us: A Memoir of Race, Beauty, and Belonging*. New York: W.W. Norton & Co., 2006.

Rosengarten, Theodore. *All God's Dangers: The Life of Nate Shaw*. New York: Alfred A. Knopf, 1974.

Ryan, Kay. *Synthesizing Gravity: Selected Prose*. New York: Grove Press, 2020.

Smith, Patti. *Just Kids*. USA: Ecco Paperback/Harper Collins, 2009.

Stein, Gertrude. *The Autobiography of Alice B. Toklas*. New York: Penguin Press, 1933/2020.

Tan, Amy. *Where the Past Begins: A Writer's Memoir*. New York: Harper Collins, 2017.

Ward, Jesmyn. *Men We Reaped: A Memoir*. New York: Bloomsbury, 2019.

Westover, Tara. *Educated: A Memoir*. New York: Penguin Random House, 2018.

Wiesel, Elie. *Night*. New York: Hill & Wang/Bantam Books, 1960.

Yogananda, Paramahansa. *The Autobiography of a Yogi*. Los Angeles: Self Realization Fellowship, 1946.

Yalom, Irvin. *Becoming Myself: A psychiatrist's memoir*. New York: Basic Books, 2017.

Yonsafzai, Malala. *I Am Malala: The Girl Who Stood Up For Education And Was Shot By The Taliban*. New York: Little, Brown and Company, 2013.

BOOKS TO HELP YOUR CLIENTS WITH THEIR WRITING

Birren, James, and Kathryn Cochran. *Telling the Stories of Life Through Guided Autobiography Groups.* Baltimore: Johns Hopkins University Press, 2001.

Cameron, Julia. *The Right to Write.* New York: Jeremy P. Tarcher/Putman, 1998.

Campbell, Richard, and Cheryl Svensson. *Writing Your Legacy: The step-by-step guide to crafting your life story.* Cincinnati, Ohio: Writer's Digest Books, 2015.

Goldberg, Natalie. *Writing Down the Bones.* Berkeley: Shambhala Books, 1986.

Lamott Anne. *Bird by Bird.* New York: Anchor Books, 1995.

Rainer, Tristine. *Your Life as Story.* New York: Jeremy P. Tarcher/Putman, 1997.

Ueland, Brenda *If You Want to Write.* Saint Paul: Graywolf Press, 1938.

Yagoda, Ben. *Memoir: A History.* New York: Riverhead Books, 2009.

WORKS CITED

Arrien, Angeles. *The Four-Fold Way: Walking the Paths of the Warrior, Teacher, Healer, and Visionary*. New York: Harper Collins Publisher, 1993.

Baikie, Karen and Kay Wilhem. 2005. Emotional and physical health benefits of expressive writing. *Advances in Psychiatric Treatment*, Vol. 11. http://apt.rcpsych.org/

Baikie, Karen and Kay Wilhelm. 2018. *Advances in Psychiatric Treatment* vol. 11, 338–346

Published online by Cambridge University Press:02 January 2018. https://www.cambridge.org/core/journals/advances-in-psychiatric-treatment/article/emotional-and-physical-health-benefits-of-expressive-writing/ED2976A61F5DE56B46F07A1CE9EA9F9F

Birren, James E., and Kathryn Cochran. *Telling the Stories of Life Through Guided Autobiography Groups*. Baltimore Maryland: Johns Hopkins University Press, 2001.

Brown, Nina W. *Psychoeducational Groups: Process and Practice*. 4th ed. New York: Routledge, 2018.

Cameron, Julia. *The Artist's Way: A Spiritual Path to Higher Creativity*. New York: Jeremy P.Tarcher/Putnam, 1992. (https://juliacameronlive.com/the-artists-way/

Cook, Barbara. *It takes nothing away from me to give to you*. Performed by Barbara Cook on the album Barbara Cook at Carnegie Hall, 1996.

Frost, Seena. *Soulcollage: An Intuitive Collage Process for Individuals and Groups*. Santa Cruz, CA: Hanford Mead Publishers, 2001.

Frost, Seena. *SoulCollage Evolving: An intuitive Collage Process for Self-Discovery and Community*. Santa Cruz, CA: Hanford Mead Publishers, 2010.

Peck, M. Scott. *The Road Less Traveled*. New York: Simon & Schuster, Inc., 1978.

Pennebaker, James and Joshua Smyth. *Opening Up by Writing It Down, How Expressive Writing Improves Health and Eases Emotional Pain*, 3rd ed. New York: The Guilford Press, 2016.

Pennebaker, J.W. and S.Beall. 1986. Confronting a traumatic event: Toward an understanding of inhibition and disease. *Journal of Abnormal Psychology* 95, 274-281.

Pennebaker, James. https://liberalarts.utexas.edu/psychology/faculty/pennebak

Phillips, Jan. Finding the On-Ramp to Your Spiritual Path: A Roadmap to Joy and Rejuvenation. Quest Books, Theosophical Publishing House, Wheaton, Illinois, 2013.

Progoff, Ira. *At a Journal Workshop: Writing to Access the Power of the Unconscious and Evoke Creative Ability*. New York: Tarcher/Putnam, 1975.

Progoff Journal Workshop (https://intensivejournal.org/Intensive_quick-summary.php).

Soghomonian, Ida. The Resilience Centre, Sydney, Australia. https://www.theresiliencecentre.com.au/boundaries-why-are-they-important/

Stone, Hal and Sidra Stone. Extensive writings to review. Delos-inc.com.

https://delos-inc.com/reading-stone.htm

Weiss, Rabbi Eric and Mishkan Aveilut. *Where Grief Resides*. Central Conference of American Rabbis. New York, 2019.

Yalom, Irving D. *The Theory and Practice of Group Psychotherapy*, 4th Ed., Basic Books, Perseus Books Group, 1995.

ACKNOWLEDGMENTS

From Bonnie.

Thank you to so many participants in the more than 75 workshops I offered and to which some people came more than thirty or forty times, supporting this process, exploration, and discovery. One group of physicians came back multiple times to consider and imagine what might enrich their lives. In the process, my life, work, and heart were filled and expanded.

Thank you to James Hagan, J.D., Ph.D., my dear friend, and guardian angel over many years.

Thank you to Hal Stone, Ph.D. and Sidra Stone, Ph.D., my teachers, and my chosen family, who gave me what matters.

A profound thank you goes to Francine Toder, Ph.D., my longtime pal, an endless contributor who shepherded this book through many iterations. This book would not be here today without her.

Of course, my life partner, Gary Embler, stayed the course in endless ways. Thank you so much.

Thank you to my devoted partner, Cheryl Svensson, from day one of GAB classes to today, through thick and thin. What a ride!

From Cheryl.

There is one person who has made this book possible – Bonnie Bernell. Bonnie, your creative spirit and questioning mind are the heart and soul of *Uncovering Treasures That Matter*.

ABOUT THE AUTHORS

For more than forty years, Bonnie Bernell has been a licensed Psychologist and is currently in private practice in Redwood City, California, and via telehealth. She is the recipient of the Distinguished Contributor to Psychology Award from the California Psychological Association and the author of the award-winning book *Bountiful Women*. For 25 years, she was an adjunct Professor of Psychology in the graduate programs at the Institute of Transpersonal Psychology, Palo Alto, CA, and at Santa Clara University, Santa Clara, CA teaching Law and Ethics, Human Sexuality. She has offered multiple continuing education classes and written in the professional literature, including as coauthor with Sandra Borrelli-Kerner, a chapter in a book edited by Randolph Charlton, M.D. and Irv Yalom, M.D., *Treating sexual disorders*, "Couple therapy of sexual disorders." She has a doctorate and a master's degree in counseling from Lehigh University, Bethlehem, Pennsylvania, and a bachelor's degree in psychology, from the University of Wisconsin, Madison. She is a member of the American Psychological Association, the California Psychological Association, the Santa Clara County Psychological Association, and the San Mateo County Psychological Association. She is an Advanced Clinician and Workshop Presenter for Imago International and is a Guided Autobiography facilitator. She is an artist—painter, and bookmaker. She currently lives in Redwood City, California, with her life partner and Brodie Lee Terrier, a border terrier. See her website at BonnieBernell.com.

Cheryl Svensson has been involved in the field of aging since she graduated from the first Masters in Gerontology program at the University of Southern California (USC) in 1977 and later completed her Ph.D. at the University of Lund, Sweden. She worked closely with Dr. James Birren, founding Dean of the Davis School of Gerontology at USC, and is the Director of the Birren Center for Autobiographical Studies (www.guidedautobiography.com). This organization is dedicated to researching and developing programs to help people write their life stories. She has taught Guided Autobiography (GAB) at USC, UCLA, and several universities, libraries, and senior and assisted living centers. In 2009 she created a live, interactive online training webinar to teach students how to become GAB instructors; there are now 600 GAB instructors in 31 countries. She is the co-author with Richard Campbell of the book, *Writing Your Legacy: The step-by-step guide to crafting your life story*. She's passionate about writing and sharing life stories. Cheryl makes her home bi-continentally – living in the fast lane in southern California and the bike lane in Sweden. You may reach her at cheryl.svensson@gmail.com.